Love, Hope & Recovery

*If your life and relationships have deteriorated
because of chemical dependency, this book
is specifically for you. It is for all
who have lived through devastating pain
in search for serenity.*

*With hope, dedication, and love, I share with you
my new life, my personal achievements, and
the joy of my life in recovery.*

"Joann's sensitive portrayal of her personal story mixed with the knowledge she has gained over the years as an alcohol and drug counselor and educator . . . will help many people find their way to treatment and recovery."

—Hillary Larsen, MS, NCAC II
Executive Director, Buckley House Programs, Inc.

"If you love someone in chemical bondage, Joann's candid disclosures will give you an advanced education on the tactics and strategies he or she might use to deny their problems and escape help. You'll learn how they think; you'll understand the anguish they're trying to hide; you'll be better equipped to counter their destructive behavior."

—Chris Adsit, Director, Disciplemakers International

"Joann understands, as does her family, that sobriety isn't about quitting something, that sobriety isn't about setting something aside. She understands that sobriety is about starting something; sobriety is about change; sobriety is about dealing with and containing that personality born of addiction so that growth can happen."

—from the Preface by Sam Graves
former Treatment Director, Serenity Lane

"I have known Joann Breeden all of her adult life and can attest to the multitude of major crises she has had to deal with before and after recovery. It is beautiful to behold the impact of her recovery on members of her family, as well as other needy families. I would recommend her book, *Love, Hope & Recovery*, to anyone who is in any way exposed to the disease of alcoholism."

—T.A. Kerns, Medical Director
Serenity Lane, Substance Abuse Treatment Center

"Joann's story is a wonderful inspiration to anyone who has ever hoped for or experienced the miracle of recovery from alcoholism and all its pain. The healing process that Joann describes for herself and her family provides hope and encouragement that change is indeed possible. This book is produced out of Joann's special caring for others and her unselfish willingness to share her story with those who may still be suffering."

—Ginny Pecora, R.N.
Administrator, Oregon Eye Surgery Center

"During the past eight years, I've heard many stories about the miracle of recovery, but few have been delivered with such impact. Joann's victories over the disease of alcoholism, and as an author, are well deserved."

—Jerry Schmidt, Director of Marketing
Serenity Lane Health Services

"The reader will find this work to be a comprehensive handbook for families dealing with chemical dependency. Whether used within an existing treatment therapy, or used to develop a new strategy, *Love, Hope & Recovery* offers the guidance and groundwork to assist families in determining their readiness to make a commitment to long-term sobriety."

—Rev. Joseph Black, M.A., N.CC., L.P.C.

"This book takes you on a journey from the unknowing darkness of addiction through the change and struggle to the light of renewed love for self and family. Joann's personal story inspires, while uncloaking some of the mystery surrounding treatment and recovery. It's a compelling story for all who want to learn about the illness we call alcoholism."

—Steve Gallon, Ph.D., Serenity Lane

"Love, Hope & Recovery is a stirring account of the defeats, triumphs, and ultimately the healing of a family racked by the insidious disease of alcoholism. This book allows the reader to experience the real life drama of people who, on the verge of total collapse, found hope and help.

"Joann's personal and honest accounting of her own life and death struggles and that of her family is profoundly touching and evokes the deepest emotions while providing clinical insights and timely information regarding substance abuse, treatment, and recovery. I highly recommend this book for professionals and non-professionals alike. . . .

"Love, Hope & Recovery speaks to the heart of any-one who has been affected by the craziness and heart-ache associated with chemical dependency."
—Lance McDonald, Ed.D., Licensed Psychologist

"This book will open your heart. Joann Breeden's story of personal and family recovery will inspire others to risk their own healing journey."
—David Stout, M.S.W., L.C.S.W.
Clinical Supervisor, Serenity Lane

LOVE, HOPE & RECOVERY

HEALING THE PAIN OF ADDICTION

JOANN E. BREEDEN

Foreword by Sharon Wegscheider-Cruse

Blue Dolphin Publishing, Inc.
1994

Published by Blue Dolphin Publishing, Inc.
P.O. Box 1920, Nevada City, CA 95959
Orders: 1-800-643-0765

ISBN: 0-931892-77-5

Library of Congress Cataloging-in-Publication Data

Breeden, Joann E., 1934-
    Love, hope, and recovery / by Joann E. Breeden.
        p. cm.
    ISBN 0-931892-77-5 : $12.95
    1. Substance abuse—Popular works. 2. Alcoholics—
Rehabilitation. 3. Drug addicts—Rehabilitation.
    4. Interpersonal relations. 5. Denial (Psychology)
    6. Recovering alcoholics—Family relationships.
    7. Recovering addicts—Family relationships. I. Title.
RC564.29.B74 1994
362.29'18—dc20   93-36924
                                                            CIP

Situations, details, and names pertaining to individuals mentioned in this book are true, but identifying characteristics have been changed for privacy and confidentiality.

Cover art by the author, Joann Breeden

Printed in the United States of America by
Blue Dolphin Press, Inc., Grass Valley, California

10   9   8   7   6   5   4   3   2   1   5M

DEDICATION

WITH ALL THE LOVE IN MY HEART, I dedicate this book to my loving family. It is dedicated especially to my husband John, who stood by me throughout the devastating years of my disease, chemical dependency, supporting me with his love and encouragement. This book is also for our three children, Renae and her husband Jon, Lorene and her husband Roché, and Don and his wife Tracy. This loving list includes my grandchildren Julia, Rachel, Laura, Annie, Kekoa, Talitha, Ikaika, Mahala, Christopher, and Andrew.

My family lived through the destructive effects of a dysfunctional home and were a vital part of my recovery. Together we are healing the painful wounds of our family disease. Together we are united and a happy family, with love and respect for each other. Without my family's love and courage I would never have found meaningful recovery. My love, my thanks, and my prayers honor them.

PERSONAL THANKS

IT IS DIFFICULT TO EXPRESS gratitude to my special friends for their reassurance and support through the many years of recovery, but it is worth the effort to try. It is comforting to know that they are always willing to give me direction and insight, to offer their love, strength, and friendship. Even though some of my friends are no longer close by, I know their love and spirit are continually with me. My thanks and appreciation to all of them for being there for me.

Joann, author, and husband, John

CONTENTS

FOREWORD

$L_{OVE,}$ $H_{OPE,}$ $_{AND}$ $R_{ECOVERY}$ is a book that needs to be read by every family that has been touched by chemical dependency. In the early 1980s I wrote a book called *Another Chance,* which was an accumulation of the work that I had done throughout the 70s and up to 1980. Over the years I learned that any family in which there has been a chemical addiction is a family that needs to learn how to put the pieces back together again. The pain of living in a dysfunctional home has touched many a person who has gone on to develop an addiction of their own. The good news is that, as families recover, they oftentimes are better off than they have ever been before. It is through people's brave sharing and their willingness to share those stories that we have found a way to heal families and bring about inner peace and serenity.

This very personal book, written by Joann Breeden, courageously shares the nightmare of addiction and then tackles the challenge: what does recovery mean? She walks the readers through the steps of finding help, of hanging on to the possibilities, of facing the challenges of recovery, of being willing to do the daily work of rebuilding relationships, and of healing love, so that individuals, families, children, and grandchildren once again have the opportunity to interrupt their cycle of pain and heal. I believe the greatest gift we can leave to our children and our grandchildren is to be willing to look at our histories and at what brought us to the point of seeking help. By unraveling family systems, family rules, and family struggles, and by rearranging priorities and decisions, we are able to offer to both our children and our grandchildren a healthier way of life.

If you yourself have struggled with addiction, take this journey with Joann and move yourself to a new level of healing. If someone you love is struggling with addiction, this book could reach them and help them begin their journey of recovery. If you are a child or a grandchild of an alcoholic, take a walk through Joann's journey and come to a new understanding, acceptance, forgiveness, and respect for the person in your life who has walked the struggle of addiction. If you are a professional, this book can help many of your clients.

It has been said that it is very, very difficult for any of us to really change the world and perhaps, in big dramatic ways, that is true, but if each one of us tells our story as Joann has so richly done in this book, there will be little parts in our world that will change. When all of these little parts add up, as people tell their stories, then the world will be changed.

Thank you, Joann, for doing your part by telling your story.

Sincerely,

Sharon Wegscheider-Cruse

PREFACE

JOANN BREEDEN is a wonderful person, a wife, a mother, a daughter, a grandmother, and a friend. Each word describes a truly unique and loving individual—sometimes complex, sometimes perfectionistic, sometimes controlling, but always dedicated to recovery.

Joann's family can attest to her addiction, the illness that has touched them all. They can also attest to the new and ugly personality that is born out of addiction, a personality that cannot be controlled, a personality that, when it reaches its full potential, is so destructive that nothing can survive in its wake.

Her family and friends can also speak about the dedication of this loving, caring, intense, creative, enthusiastic, and motivated woman who understands there is more to recovery than just setting aside her drug of choice. Joann understands, as does her family, that sobriety isn't about quitting something, that sobriety isn't about setting something aside. She understands that sobriety is about starting something, sobriety is about change, sobriety is about dealing with and containing that personality born of addiction so that growth can happen.

With the support of a very loving and forgiving family, Joann has spent years pursuing acceptance of self and others, restoring trust, overcoming childhood issues, and developing the kinds of relationships that can only come from a family in recovery.

Joann has grown in many ways, not only as an individual, but as a fine family counselor who has helped many others experience the reward of wellness. She helped develop the family program at Serenity Lane addiction treatment center; she presented or directed many one-day and five-day wellness workshops for alumni, and the list goes on.

She also discovered many talents as sobriety took root. Along with love and caring for other people, her family, and her God, she has also become a wonderful artist, an accomplished tennis player, and now an author. This is a wonderful book by a lovely lady.

Sam Graves,
former Treatment Director, Serenity Lane

*Counselor Sam Graves and
Joann's husband, John*

INTRODUCTION

LOVE, HOPE, AND RECOVERY is specifically written to assist anyone willing to restore relationships affected by the disease of chemical dependency. It is my hope, by sharing my personal experiences of life, the constant pain, the desperation and struggles, which occurred before and after treatment for my alcoholism, that new insights and hope will be given to others. I want families to understand that they, too, can recover from this destructive disease, just as my family has done.

One goal of this book is to relate the new opportunities and joys that are available in recovery. Another goal is to show that trust and positive change is possible when we work for it. It is important to understand that we can rise above despair, even while dealing with the daily trauma of living with the disease of addiction. If we want recovery, it is each individual's responsibility to initiate personal healing and to examine new choices. Many of those who live with the harmful disease don't fully realize that they can recover—that they *can* have a healthier life.

The stories in my book are true and make up a small piece of my history, told just as I remember parts of my life.

In some instances, I have tried to show the distortions of my limited vision and the ways that I complicated my life with my addiction and damaging behavior.

Love, Hope, and Recovery illustrates that it is possible to renew love and to trust, just as my family found the love we thought was lost. It is essential to recognize and talk about feelings, and to have good communication, for a healthy recovery. Learning and practicing new living skills, along with developing positive self-esteem, helped our family immensely. In order to have a meaningful recovery and find peace, my dysfunctional family had to adapt various new methods of living.

The many miracles and personal rewards my family has found are emphasized in this book. The price of recovery is ongoing, consistent hard work, which takes time. Faith in God, oneself, and others is most important in recovery. Faith renews hopes and dreams as it heals our souls. We need faith to conquer the disease of addiction and to help us realize that life can be so much better than dying.

At the back of the book, I have provided a workbook section which includes specific self-help exercises that I have used through the years. During my seventeen years in the counseling field, I have learned that people want specific skills to help them achieve their objectives.

My book, a gift of hope and love, is especially written for all individuals who want recovery. I firmly believe those who read my book about our family's remarkable recovery will benefit a great deal.

There are times when I think back on the living hell, the miserable existence of my personal nightmare, and wonder how I ever managed to escape my destructive downward spiral in the grip of chemical dependency. At the same time, I shudder inside when I recall how close to death I came on several suicidal occasions. To come back from the living dead into a joyful life full of promise and personal rewards is really a miracle. To know that I can now live my life in a meaningful way, rather than destructively, is truly a blessing.

It is my hope that this book conveys the excitement of recovery that my family experienced in our battle with the disease of alcoholism. Each day I am filled with wonder at my good fortune to be alive, with many new challenges and opportunities before me. I am eternally grateful that God touched my life in such remarkable ways. Without God's love and help, my relationship with my marvelous husband and my extraordinary children would never have been renewed, nor would I have experienced the joys of my grandchildren. Without God, sharing my life and recovery with you could never have happened.

My gift to you is my book of hope, of happiness, and of personal strength to assist you in your search for love and inner peace.

Joann Breeden, C.A.D.C.

Part One

Joann and John

1

ENDING OF A NIGHTMARE

As I LOOKED IN THE MIRROR, a pathetic vision of misery stared back. There was so much despair and anguish written on my face that I had to look away. My skin was drained of color and my dark hair lying across the pillow was the only contrast to the stark white walls and hospital sheets. Although I was in the hospital as a result of a fall, I kept thinking about my painful existence. Why did I feel so completely miserable and worthless as a human being? How was it possible that I had descended the road of self-destruction to certain disaster without stopping myself? What was wrong with me that I couldn't put my life together? There were no answers for me, at least any that I wanted to hear or accept.

While lying in the hospital bed, I noticed a hideous skin rash had developed on my arms from the antiseptic sheets. With growing dismay, I further examined my thin, unhealthy body. In the past two years I had lost a lot of weight, since food held no interest for me anymore. Weighing less than one hundred pounds wasn't enough for my five-foot-four-inch frame. Then I recalled my previous experiences in these havens for the sick. The few times I had formerly been a hospital patient, something dreadful usually happened to me. Little did I know that my pessimistic prediction was about to become a reality once again.

For hours I lay in my uncomfortable bed, feeling lost and lonely, with no visitors or phone calls to cheer me up. Suddenly, I heard whispering voices from the hall, so I wiped away my tears, waiting for my company to enter the room. It was probably my family; I didn't have any close friends anymore.

When the door opened, my husband John, our three children, my parents and Dr. Kerns, our family doctor, entered. No one said anything, nor did they glance at me as they quietly filed into the room. Somehow I knew something was dreadfully wrong when I looked at the somber group circling the foot of my bed. Their worried faces looked grim as they avoided looking into my searching eyes.

There was no attempt to hug me or offer condolences, so naturally I concluded that I must have some horrifying, terminal disease. Even though for years I had wanted to die, it was scary to finally realize that my time was up. Dr. Kerns spoke first, "Hello Joann. Sorry to barge in like this." In his flat, monotone voice, he continued, "Joann, your family has some things they want to talk to you about. They're concerned about you and your declining health. I understand that you don't exercise at all, or eat properly. Your entire body is deteriorating." His words sank in, tightening my stomach as if it had been hit with a baseball bat. Shocked, I knew my fate was worse than anything I had ever imagined.

Immediately it became clear to me what the gathering was all about. I knew I had been a terrible wife and mother for years, but to punish me so severely for my inadequacies was completely unfair. Panic set in as I realized that my family wished to put me away in an institution. My first thought was, "What a lousy trick, to descend upon me when I'm sick and at their mercy." And then I thought, "They want to commit me to avoid being around me."

My husband, with tears in his eyes and his voice shaking with pain, spoke next, "I care about you, Joann, but I've finally reached my limit. I want you to get help for your drinking, but if you don't, I won't stay around any more and watch you die. I didn't know what else to do, so I went to Dr. Kerns for help." Wiping away his tears, he struggled through the difficult words, "For too many years, I stood by, hoping for a miracle, but our misery only grew worse. It hurts deeply to watch our family being destroyed, to witness our children suffering so much pain. Maybe it's too late, but I can no longer ignore our misery." Even in my angry state, the agony in his face was unbearable to watch. Inside, I knew that I'd put him through hell. Closing my eyes, I stuffed my guilt deep into my pit of despair and concealed it with my solid wall of denial.

Indeed, I knew what this "meeting" was all about. A few months ago I had read one of the brochures that John had conveniently left around the house. It mentioned a family gathering called an "intervention, a time when family and friends lovingly attempt to convince a person to get help for addictions." Not only did my family want to imprison me, but they expected me to quit using alcohol. Even though I had assured them many times that I didn't have a problem with alcohol, it seemed they didn't believe me. I knew that Dr. Kerns had recently started a treatment center for alcoholics, so I suspected my family intended to put me there.

When John finished pouring out his heart and soul, he sat down, exhausted. Then each of our children, Renae, Lorene, and Don, gathered their strength one by one and told me of their distress. Crying in pain, Renae said, "I love you, Mom, even though it has been hard to at times." My son Don, weeping, pleaded with me, "I don't want you to die." Lorene told me, "You need some help, Mom." I couldn't stand watching their raw emotion much longer. It took all of my remaining stamina to keep from completely falling apart: there, next to my silent, disapproving father, was my mother sobbing and saying, "Please, Joann, go to treatment."

Even though so much pain and emotion was being expressed, I was determined not to go along with their plans. I was furious about my situation and with their condemning words. Against my will, my defenses seemed to be eroding. I was ashamed that my life had come to this terrible moment. Although my determined family wouldn't give up, all I could think about was escaping from the hospital to a place where they couldn't get me. The doctor kept the pressure on. One by one, my family elaborated in more painful detail about my ongoing battle with alcohol and how they witnessed our family falling apart.

I only half-listened and argued vigorously with them, but in vain. My family's pain suffocated me, penetrating my very soul. I could see no way out; I could stand no more. To appease them, I finally agreed to go into a treatment center for my drinking (I couldn't call myself alcoholic yet). "But," I said, "only after the summer is over. I'm too busy right now." My excuses fell on deaf ears. In desperation I attempted another diversion. I told them, with tears of anguish streaming down my cheeks now, "I'll go to treatment, but only after I go home for some clothes." They didn't accept that flimsy excuse either. It was as if they didn't have any trust in me, as if they knew of my plan to desert as soon as I left the hospital.

Little by little, John, the doctor, and my children whittled away my resistance until I was completely exhausted. I finally gave up and said, "You win. I'll go now." Without hesitation my family responded, giving me a choice of two live-in treatment centers. One was out of town, where I would be given alcohol for ten days, along with injections of a substance that caused vomiting. This was called Aversion Treatment. The other was a program in my home town of Eugene, Oregon, that lasted for eight weeks.

I thought, "Big deal, some choice." Although the longer treatment sounded like an eternity, I hated the idea of throwing up for any length of time, so I agreed to go to the facility in Eugene. I sighed in defeat, trapped. Then the flame of defiance leapt again and I shouted, "If I go I want to wear my own clothes!" And with one sweep of my arm I sent the contents of my bedside tray flying.

Unimpressed, Dr. Kerns said, "Fine, have it your way." Then John handed me my jeans and sweater and said, "Joann, clean up this mess before we go." Furious, I grabbed my clothes and ran into the bathroom to change and hide from their overpowering pain. I didn't feel like I was getting my way, but at least they agreed to let me leave the hospital with a shred of dignity.

We left the hospital, and all the way to the treatment center I continued to rage silently, desperately trying to figure out how I could run away. Since the Center was only five blocks from the hospital, I didn't have much time to think of an escape plan. No traffic lights held us up and I was afraid to jump from a moving car. We arrived before I could decide what to do. Trying to distract me, the doctor told me the name of the treatment center was "Serenity Lane." Disbelieving, I said, "You've got to be kidding!" I couldn't accept that I would be imprisoned in a place with a ridiculous name like that. Even in this bleak hour, the irony of the name did not escape me. My laughter was as bitter as my tears.

After playing the game of me locking and the doctor unlocking the car several times in front of the Center, he finally beat me to one door before I secured it. Since there was heavy afternoon traffic passing by, I was afraid someone would see me walking into this "terrible" place. Dr. Kerns, who was a lot bigger than me, had to pry me out of his car. Then he firmly pushed me through the front door. Without a doubt, going through that door of reality was one of the hardest things I have ever done. I trembled with humiliation and shame for myself and my situation. It was impossible to hold back my tears anymore.

After the determined Dr. Kerns literally pushed me up the stairs to the second floor, I suffered the indignities of the "admission process." To make matters worse, the head nurse, Mary Ann, who I knew from my high school days, greeted me like a long lost friend. Smiling, she said, "Oh, Joann, I'm so glad to see you," as if she expected me. The cheerful nurses were quite nice to me during and after check-in, but I didn't think they had any right asking me such personal questions and writing it all in a chart for others to see. Whose business was it but mine how often I went to the bathroom, or how many times my husband and I fought or made love? Besides putting up with this invasion of privacy, I had to contend with the persistent nurse's aide. We wrestled for my personal belongings for ten minutes. She wanted me to trade my clothes for a set of enormous pajamas and robe.

Following the "processing," I endured a physical exam, then the nurse assigned me to a room across from the nurse's station so the staff could keep an eye on me. Fortunately, no one occupied the other bed, so I would at least have some privacy. After thoroughly checking the windows for an escape route, I concluded that even thin as I was, I couldn't fit through the small opening in the window. Apparently they had thought of everything short of bars on the window to keep me prisoner.

I was so angry and mortified about being there that I wouldn't leave my room for several days, but this didn't stop those happy little nurses. With perpetual smiles, they continually invaded my privacy. Popping into my room unannounced, they inquired about my condition and whether I was happy. It was a stupid question. Of course I wasn't happy. My heartless family had just left me there to fend for myself. To make matters worse, I was embarrassed to learn that I knew several people on the staff. I thought, "The word will be out now. Everyone will know where I am." (I didn't realize that the staff couldn't disclose the names of patients to people on the "outside.") Their expressions of delight at seeing me and their enthusiasm about this wonderful, highly-regarded treatment center did nothing to cheer me up. Instead, I sat in my room, brooding about my misfortune and about how cruel my family was to me.

Then, the day after admission, a smiling man with an out-of-date crew cut came bounding into my room. I thought, "Heaven help me, not another one of these cheery types." By this time my room wasn't much different than Grand Central Station, with people coming and going at will. Grinning from ear to ear, the man with the funny hair said his name was Sam and that he was to be my counselor. With perseverance, he tried his best to get me to talk with him, but I punished him with my finest scowl. He inquired, "How are you doing?"

I mumbled, "Lousy."

Trying again, he said, "You'll feel better in a few days." Instead of acknowledging him, I gave him my most withering look of disgust, reprimanding him with silence. What he said next caught me totally off guard. With a twinkle in his eye he mischievously offered, "I'll make a deal with you. I won't rape you if you won't rape me." Completely taken by surprise, I looked at him with astonishment and burst out laughing. But even though I had allowed my guard to slip, I quickly returned to my mood of dark despair. I was beside myself with fear of the unknown: what was to become of me? My treatment had begun.

2

FINDING HOPE—FINDING HELP

SINCE MY FAMILY had forced me to go into treatment, I wasn't pleased about being in what was described as a "highly-acclaimed alcoholism treatment center." Following my admission to Serenity Lane, many avenues of flight crossed my troubled mind. I thought of calling friends to assist my escape, but I wasn't close to anyone anymore. Running down the stairs, out the door, and down the street in my pajamas didn't appeal to me either. Somehow my energy for active resistance had completely disappeared. Despair grew instead. There was nowhere to go or hide, except in my room, so I could sulk alone. It seemed this was the end of my life: I might as well give up.

To my dismay, the head nurse, Mary Ann, greeted me each morning with cheerful anticipation of good things to come, as if we were residents of the Beverly Hills Hilton. In order to short circuit my negativity and make my arrival at the Center seem more joyous, Mary Ann exclaimed one day, "You are so lucky, Joann! It just happens to be the Center's first year birthday celebration. And guess what? You get to be a part of it."

Dejected, I thought sarcastically, "Thrill, thrill, just what I always wanted to do." However, I didn't have a choice of whether I went to the party or not, since the staff required all the patients to attend the festivities. Besides being a reunion of former patients and sponsors of the Center, patients were given a chance to get to know other people in recovery. Excuses of being near death didn't seem to matter. "Besides," I argued, "I've just come from the hospital and my hair is a mess. In any event, I can't possibly go to the party, especially in those unattractive pajamas and robe that you require me to wear." As usual, the staff went on with their business as if I hadn't said a word.

A short while later, nurse Mary Ann brought an energetic and extremely persuasive woman with graying short hair into my room. Her name was Lois, spelled "I-can-talk-you-into-anything, and-I-will." And she did. Not only did she persuade me to attend the party, but she pleasantly chatted with me about how wonderful it was for me to be here in the best treatment program in the country. As I rolled my eyes heavenward, I thought, "Give me strength, another Pollyanna to deal with." The staff seemed to think Serenity Lane was some kind of special reward for drunks. Although I learned that Lois could function in any of the staff's many roles, her primary job was Receptionist and Patient Admissions at Serenity Lane.

In my agitated state, I had considerable doubts about this place being "wonderful." I was in no mood to agree with her. Yet, no matter how much I discounted her, Lois's enthusiasm remained undaunted. She just went right on ruining my wish to be miserable. Undiscouraged, she vowed, "You will soon love it here. It's the greatest treatment center in the world." Cynically, I thought, "Whippee dee, I'm soooo lucky." All the while Lois was trying to cheer me up, she magically arranged my hair so I no longer looked like a scarecrow. Try as I would, it was difficult to be disagreeable around her. It was the beginning of my growing respect and loving affection for this radiantly happy woman.

At first I didn't realize how truly unusual Lois was. She had the qualities that I wanted in a mother. She was warm, sincere, considerate, loving, and had a great sense of humor. Her beauty radiated both inside and outside. Being hugged by her was like the embrace of a warm and loving teddy bear. During the weeks to come, Lois reminisced about her childhood and the parents she had been blessed with. She had a particularly close relationship with her mother. Enviously I wished that my mother and I could have experienced the same warm and open relationship.

As our friendship grew, our discussions deepened into the personal. She was so easy to talk to that I found myself sharing things I had never told another person before. As we talked about our inner thoughts and feelings, my protective barriers lowered. I gained fresh insights into myself. Areas I had thought barren began to put forth tiny tendrils of new growth. Little roots of new emotional strengths were put down during those long talks together and the day came when I saw that I did have some good qualities. It was like seeing a tender green for the first time after a long winter, to realize, through Lois, that I truly loved and cared about people and was sensitive to their needs. She helped me to see my compassionate and loving side, which for too long had been buried beneath my disease of alcoholism.

One of the first things I learned during treatment is that there are people who come from a healthy family system. Not all families are dysfunctional, rigid, and need-deprived. Even though I didn't grow up in a family where love and feelings were openly shared, I discovered that I could develop a happier life for myself. It was okay to acquire substitute family members in my friends and reach out to them whenever I needed to. I adopted Lois as my first substitute mother and another close friend, my hairdresser, Flo, as my second substitute mother. When I first asked Flo to fix my hair at the Center it was difficult, but she came willingly and without judgment. Her many strong qualities seem to shine from within, through her blue eyes, sparkling with constant energy. She had many strong qualities that showed in her face, which glowed with kindness whenever she spoke. Each time she laughed, her short blond hair bounced as if delighted. Flo had a radiance and gentleness about her that touched me deeply. Whenever I shared a problem with her or asked for advice, she was willing to be direct with me. Her wisdom and personal inner strength, along with her love and intuitive insight, were there when I needed them. I never knew from what well she drew her happiness, but its abundance quenched many a thirst in me over the years.

My background differed from that of my two adoptive "moms," but it didn't mean that I couldn't change my life. Each day in treatment I learned about many new choices that were available to me. For one, I could find better ways to communicate and share feelings. Another choice was to be more loving and not so self-centered. A third option was either to research my past or avoid dealing with it. Fourth and most crucial, I could recover or relapse. All I had to do was take the risk of moving forward, but that was the terrifying part, taking risks. One of the risks that frightened me was asking for guidance, reaching out and saying, "I need help." All my life I had had problems asking for assistance. I couldn't express my desires, fearing my incompetencies would be revealed and others would think I was stupid. The fear of rejection was overwhelming and kept me isolated from friends. Since I didn't have a positive self-image, I thought people weren't interested in me and that they wouldn't want to help me.

Since my room at the Center was close to the nurse's station, the constant noise kept me from getting much sleep. One time I peeked out of my room and nearly passed out from fright. Before me stood a ruddy, stubble-faced, hairy zombie, dressed in the usual hospital attire. Harold, a new patient, stared at me with completely red eyes that looked like they were on wrong side out. He looked so dreadful that I wondered how anyone could look that bad and actually be alive.

Another time, I heard a terrible ruckus in the hall. A huge man named Mick, going through an alcoholic hallucination, was making noises resembling an engine running loudly. It seems he thought he was driving a truck. With his hands in front of him encircling an imaginary steering wheel, he literally dragged several nurses and patients on his arms up and down the hall as they tried unsuccessfully to stop him. After a few hours of this, he finally ran out of gas, exhausted, and went to bed. I thought, "And I'm supposed to get better in this funny farm?" A few days later, I learned that there are some people, and Mick was one of them, who have far more difficulty going through withdrawal from alcohol or drugs than others. After witnessing this man's reaction, it was clear that I didn't want this to happen to me. I thought, "Maybe using alcohol wasn't such a good idea after all!"

Shortly after my admission, after spending several days in those chic pajamas, I was allowed to move to another room, away from the chaos of the nurse's station. I complained to Dr. Kerns, "I'm completely exhausted, living in this zoo," but I received no sympathy. In his flat voice, he offered me some encouraging words, "Nobody ever died from lack of sleep." Besides getting to move, I finally received my own clothes. The frumpy look of my hospital outfit was history. This joyous occasion was an important part of regaining my self-respect. Once I had my own clothes, I felt more secure; I felt I was moving in a new direction. Hope for the future glimmered inside of me.

However, in my new room another disappointment awaited me—a roommate. I'm shy by nature and cherish my privacy. Nonetheless, my resistance was nearly gone by now, so I grudgingly accepted my new companion. Besides, to make a fuss would have been fruitless, since there were no private rooms. As it turned out, my roommate Elaine and I got along fine. It was a relief to talk to someone who was as miserable as I was.

While I was getting settled and meeting new people who were "in" for the same thing I was, my counselor Sam wanted to talk with me about my treatment plan. With enthusiasm and a "happy with life" attitude, he explained "the fantastic things treatment offers." During orientation to the treatment program format, he told me, "You will get the opportunity to become educated about the disease of chemical dependency by attending two lectures a day." I thought, "I can handle that. Maybe this place won't be so bad after all."

"Not only that," he continued, "in order to round out your treatment, you are required to participate and attend two group sessions per day." While my heart stopped beating, he topped it off by adding that I was going to have the opportunity (they used this word a lot in treatment) to do this for eight weeks. The news completely terrified me. There was no way that I could share my heart and soul with so many strangers. It was too threatening to think about, so I insisted firmly to my counselor, "I won't have to be in treatment that long. Since I am quite intelligent, I should have everything down pat in a week, or two at the most." My desperate protest wasn't acknowledged. Sam gently but firmly went on to explain the treatment process as though I hadn't uttered a word.

Panic took hold of me and I felt my face turn gray with fear. Sam reached out and gently assured me, "Don't worry; everything will be just fine." The truth of the matter was, I wanted to bolt out the door and run the four miles home, but I just couldn't. Sam was sitting in front of the door and knew that look of wild desperation and hysteria very well.

As Sam calmed my anxiety with his caring and understanding words, I started to let my guard down. Just a bit. For the time being, I allowed myself the luxury of some trust. Sam encouraged me, "Really, 'group' isn't all that bad and you'll learn to like it." Attempting to smile, I thought, "This guy is really full of it." Once again, I was too tired to fight any longer, so I decided to go along with him, at least for awhile. "After all," I schemed, "he doesn't need to know that I'm not planning on sharing any of my pain or problems in his group."

After a few days into treatment, I came to the realization that I needed to be there. During an education lecture, it became clear that I had the disease of alcoholism. Once my denials were penetrated, I stopped fighting and resisting help. Even so, accepting the fact that I was an alcoholic was extremely difficult for me. Being trapped in an alcoholism hospital had not been on my life's agenda, yet here I was, with nowhere to go. Humbled, I began my healing journey.

Since there was no hugging or meaningful sharing of feelings in my family, I was totally unprepared for the expectations of the treatment staff for my recovery. When I first arrived at the Center I was terrified, humiliated, and completely miserable. Despite this, everyone was friendly. It was all so confusing. The staff, as well as patients, were always smiling, reaching out, and giving support when needed. At that time, I thought, "This display is completely disgusting." And the most unnerving practice was the hugging. It seemed like everyone was continually hugging one another, whether it was for comfort, acceptance, or support. Because I wasn't used to demonstrative behavior, I had an extremely difficult time accepting this unfamiliar practice. But once I stopped resisting the hugs and checked out how I felt inside, something happened. When someone offered encouragement in the form of a hug, I discovered I felt a great deal of contentment.

Reaching out to others was very hard for me at first, but after practicing a couple weeks I found it came much more easily. Throughout my life there had been many times when I wanted to reach out, yet I hadn't known how. This new manner of self-expression was fulfilling to me. Once I started getting into this new hugging habit, I never wanted to stop.

One day in the week following my admission to treatment, I learned that one of the chaplains at Serenity Lane was Monsignor Murnane. He had been my principal in high school. During those years we had had various conflicts, so I wasn't eager to have him know that I was in this shameful place. After all, he would probably smugly nod his head and indicate that he wasn't surprised in the least to see me. I heard he had appointments with patients at the Center and I was afraid I would run into him. In order to avoid his judgment, I thought it would be best if I hid in the second floor ladies' restroom in one of the stalls until he left the building.

Unbeknownst to me, when a patient is missing, the staff sends out their National Guard to search. When they found me crouched on the toilet seat lid in the women's restroom, it was a humiliating ordeal, especially after nurse Mary Ann screamed down the hall, "Here she is! Here she is!" Everyone in a five block radius knew she had found me. As I was escorted down the hall by the nurses, I hung my head in embarrassment while everyone looked at me. Then the chaplain saw me and greeted me like a long lost companion, "Joann, how good it is to see you!" I thought, "Now my hearing is going, too." It wasn't long after this episode that I learned what a truly special and dedicated man the Monsignor was. Through the years he had changed a lot and so had I. The difference was that he had grown closer to his spirituality and I had grown away from mine. At this point I decided to listen to what he had to offer, rather than resist his teachings as I had in the past.

Letting others help me and show me a better way to live was very tough to accept. The love and the care the staff gave not only to me, but to all of the patients, no matter how pathetic we might appear, was therapeutic and healing to us all. As I started to come out of myself, a whole new world of nurturing love opened up, allowing inner healing to occur.

Many people working at the treatment center were in recovery themselves. There was a different aura about them compared to other staff. An inner peace and joy appeared to illuminate them from within, a unique phenomena that I had never witnessed before. I decided I wanted that same peaceful presence for myself. At that time, I made a determined commitment to myself to search for answers and make critical changes in my life until that inner peace and contentment were mine.

However, in those days the fear of a setback continually kept me from growing emotionally. Fear of not succeeding was the ever-present excuse that kept me stuck in my misery—fear that if I took responsibility for my life, I'd have no one else to blame for my setbacks. Overcoming this enormous obstacle was a very difficult step for me, but a necessary one if I was to combat this disease of alcoholism.

Besides group therapy and lectures, part of the treatment program required patients to attend weekly Alcoholics Anonymous meetings, a support group for recovering alcoholics. I soon discovered that each AA meeting has a different format. Some are discussion meetings, others deal with the famous twelve steps of the AA program. During the AA meetings I attended, the first thing expected of me was to state my first name and then identify whether I was an alcoholic or a drug addict. Saying the words, "I am an alcoholic," did not come easy. At the first few AA meetings, my heart pounded wildly when it was my turn. After softly stating, "My name's Joann," I mumbled incoherently, "I'm an alcoholic." I was so ashamed of myself, embarrassed to admit that I was alcoholic. To me, an alcoholic was a skid row bum, not a housewife and mother like me. Though I admitted to myself that I had a problem with alcohol, I hadn't really accepted that I was alcoholic. There is a vast difference between the two.

Part of the Alcoholics Anonymous and Serenity Lane treatment philosophy is learning to be honest with oneself and others. After living a lie for so many years concerning my alcoholism, it wasn't easy to honestly look at my life and at what I'd become. Although I'd always considered myself an honest person, when I analyzed my past life it was clear that my vision had been greatly distorted.

During treatment I learned about the many facets of alcoholism. I began to see how I had used alcohol to help me feel better about myself and to numb my feelings. It was a tremendous relief for me to understand that because I was alcoholic I wasn't a "weak" person, nor was I a "bad" person. Learning that the destructive disease was nothing to be ashamed of was a momentous discovery for me.

Not only did I learn about physical dependence, but also about the psychological aspects of the disease. Information regarding genetic predisposition (that is, the passing of genes through generations) helped me to see how the disease runs in families. If I was to survive the devastating disease, it was imperative that I learn as much as possible about it.

It was remarkable how little I knew concerning the disastrous effects of the disease of addiction. It seemed that I'd lived with my head in the sand for a very long time. A new revelation for me was that the disease not only affected me, but was destroying my family, as well. They too, were a part of the disease. We were all struggling to exist together as we became emotionally ill. Although I tended to blame my family for my problems, including my drinking, I discovered in treatment that my disease was no one's fault, and no one was to blame. I could have found a variety of methods to help me deal with my problems other than using alcohol to medicate my emotions. However, alcohol had been my path; now it was completely essential for my recovery to become responsible for myself and my actions. I needed to grow up and take charge of my life.

In many ways, treatment was the beginning of adulthood for me. There had been many areas in my life where I lacked the strength and wisdom of maturity. One extremely weak area was being able to develop friendships. I was informed that I had to become involved with emotionally healthy people or my sobriety would be threatened. To begin with, it was necessary for me to become involved with other patients rather than isolate myself—but it was hard for me to socialize without alcohol to assist. Following visiting hours at the Center, the evenings became important times of reflection with other patients. We discussed ourselves, our problems, and how we were progressing in treatment. We offered insights and encouragement to each other. It was during these discussions that I started to let my guard down and allowed trust in my new friends to increase. Each moment of the day was a new part of healing, enabling me to become stronger. By now, I had found that I was not alone in my struggles. Every patient was going through similar conflicts and feelings.

Not knowing how to handle my feelings had been a major problem for me all my life. Now I was told by my counselor, Sam, that I needed to give myself approval to "feel my feelings." This was an entirely new concept to me. Telling myself that all of my feelings were genuine and that I was entitled to each one of them wasn't easy to accept. I kept reverting back to the childhood messages I'd gotten from my parents, "It's wrong to be angry, to be afraid." Then I would catch myself and have to reinforce the lesson that it was okay to feel those feelings. The payoff was that when I talked about my pain I felt better inside.

During the course of treatment I learned many other new things. Group therapy opened my eyes to various ways I had learned to manipulate other people, especially my family. To underline this awareness, Sam assigned me to research my habits and write a paper on "Manipulation."

As I wrote my thoughts, I became aware that manipulation had been my primary technique for achieving goals or fulfilling desires. Looking back through the years, I remembered several incidents. One time during my drinking years, a dance was coming up that I wanted to go to. As usual, I was afraid to tell my husband John my desire. Instead I told him, "Some of our friends are going and I thought it would be fun if we joined them." Rather than being direct with him about my needs, I used the "bandwagon technique" to maneuver him into agreeing to go. When I look back at my life, I can see that I manipulated many times so I wouldn't have to deal with disappointment and rejection.

Fear of being honest about my needs hampered my relationship with John a great deal. In recovery it was critical for me to understand and accept that "what I want" and "what I need" are important. But it is my responsibility to inform those around me what those wants are. Too often I believed that my husband could read my mind. Whenever I assumed John or any other person knew what I was thinking, I brought nothing but trouble upon myself. Each time I attempted this guessing game with my husband, it ended up eroding our relationship further.

My treatment program also provided me with other tools that I could use toward more satisfying relationships with my family. One was improved personal communication skills. I learned to take small steps at first, such as identifying my feelings and then discussing them. Also, when I truly understood and accepted that progress and change were inevitable parts of a slow process, a great deal of disappointment when changes didn't occur immediately was alleviated. I accepted a new fundamental principle of recovery, that continuous work on these skills was the only way change would happen.

Change had never been easy for me, but at that time of my life I was weary of living in misery, so I made a commitment to myself to do something more meaningful with my life. Now that I was finding hope, maybe I could change. Perhaps I could find some happiness and peace for myself.

However, during this time doubts and concerns about our family's future haunted me. Each day I asked myself, "Will it be possible to repair the emotional bitterness in our family? Will we be able to love again? How can I stay sober in a world full of drinking?" I was scared and insecure about what to do with my new life. Yet I kept hearing at Alcoholics Anonymous meetings, "You can make a new life, one day at a time." It was true that many people were staying sober. Even though I didn't know the answers to my questions, I did have a kit full of new tools to utilize. It was crucial to use what I had learned and to go slowly.

It became clear to me in treatment that I had desired acceptance from others all of my life. First I had to master accepting myself for who I am, rather than who I wanted to be. Only then could I move forward. Finally, I realized that the only one who could improve my self-image was me. No one was able to do that for me; it was my responsibility. Attempting new challenges and sharing intimacies with those in whom I learned to trust was a big step on the way to rebuilding my life. I had so much work to do. Each time I thought about the many years before me, my heart seemed to stop, allowing my fear to overwhelm me.

3

HOPE IN RECOVERY

COMPLETE TERROR describes the feeling I experienced when it came time for my first day in "group." With my stomach in knots and my heart racing, I slid into a seat in the corner of the group room. I thought that if I didn't move, the nine other people gathered in a circle of chairs wouldn't notice me. However, just sitting and listening to everyone else talk didn't go over well with my counselor. Sam firmly, yet gently (he did that a lot), informed me, "Joann, you have to get involved in the group if you are going to learn anything about yourself." I bitterly thought, "Go suck a lemon, buddy—I'm not telling my secrets to these strangers," as I smiled sweetly. Anyway, I wasn't sure I wanted to learn any more about me. What I did know wasn't all that inspiring. But, as usual, Sam got what he wanted.

The other group members seemed to have no problem being open. After someone talked about a personal problem, Sam said, "How are you feeling about that, Joann?" When I muttered, "I don't know," he came back with, "I don't know isn't acceptable." This irritating response infuriated me time and time again throughout treatment. No matter what occurred in the group, he kept coming back to me, never letting me just sit there. Sam skillfully probed, drawing me into the group. At times it was as if he could actually see every ounce of pain in my soul.

Disciplining myself to attempt new challenges without being controlled by fear of a setback was the struggle of a lifetime for me. Part of the group therapy process in treatment is to confront other group members concerning their behavior or lack of involvement when it is necessary. I remember the first time I confronted a fellow group member about interrupting others. My heart was pounding rapidly. My mouth was completely dry. My breathing was unsteady and every word seemed to stick in my throat. Fear consumed me. However, after several attempts to express my feelings, I finally verbalized my concerns. I told Sid, "I really feel frustrated when I'm interrupted. It hurts me that what I'm saying doesn't seem to be important to you." Everyone stared at me in absolute shock, not because of what I said, but because I finally spoke up in group. There was an immense inner relief when Sid didn't hit me or argue with me. Instead, he merely contemplated the information I had given him. Nobody tried to put me down or ridicule me for what I had expressed. In fact, other group members declared some concerns about the same behavior I had identified.

Recognizing my feelings was a difficult step, but an even harder one was giving myself permission to have my feelings. Sam, my counselor, told me to repeat several times a day, "It's okay to feel; it's okay to express my thoughts." After practicing I began to understand that no one has the power to control my feelings unless I give them the power. In other words, I am in charge of my emotions, with a choice in what I feel and how I deal with my feelings.

Finding words to describe emotions I had felt in the past, or was currently experiencing, was tougher than I thought. I was used to automatically suppressing my feelings. I had trouble even acknowledging them, let alone talking about feelings after becoming aware of them. At times it was overwhelmingly painful to delve into my past years of suppressed emotions, discuss them, deal with them and let them go. Sorting through my past "garbage" in treatment was hard work, especially when there was so much of it.

Since it wasn't easy to talk about feelings, I discovered it worked to practice this skill in stages. For example, one day I talked about one emotion, such as my fear, with Carol. I told her, "It really scares me when I have to talk in front of other people." The next day I spoke about my angry feelings with Al. "It makes me so angry when someone is rude," I said. It was getting easier for me, so the following day I revealed two more feelings of hurt and sadness with Janice. I told her, "It hurts a lot and makes me sad that I grew up ignorant about how to handle life." I continued the process each day for a number of weeks until it was more comfortable. Following each disclosure I checked out how I felt inside, which enabled my awareness to grow.

As I thought about my stored feelings through the years, I pictured them in "feeling sacks." For instance, if I wanted to feel sad, I could look in my sack of sad pain in order to feel pity. As the sadness came, it overwhelmed me, filling me with sympathy for my situation. Whenever I desired to be a martyr, I pulled out my martyr sack to gain compassion. If I was into my anger, I brought out my anger sack to keep people away from me. As I learned to deal with my "sacks" of emotions more appropriately, I had the option to fill them with happy and more pleasant sentiments. As a result, the joyful, positive sacks eventually became a major part of restoring healthy emotions that healed my inner spirit, heart, and body.

Every day new enlightenment in group allowed me to grow and open up. I was like a flower bud, slowly opening, revealing myself as I received nourishing sunlight. One new realization was that although I have a right to emotions, I don't have the right to take them out on someone else by hurting them in any way, nor can I medicate my feelings with alcohol anymore. Each emotion, whether it is anger, hurt, fear, or love, is legitimate. There are no "bad" feelings, no right or wrong feelings. I remembered when I was drinking, I refused to talk about my underlying pain, but would tell my husband with angry actions and words, "It's your fault I am so miserable." Now I discovered that it was *my* fault I was so miserable.

Each day treatment felt more comfortable, and it especially helped that I was accepted by my group. One day during lecture the speaker stated, "To heal, we need to know ourselves in order to find self-acceptance." If I am tired of being miserable and full of pain, then it is my responsibility to open the door to my heart by sharing those sentiments with others. For certain, I can change my misery to happiness if I choose to do so.

During the first weeks of group therapy, I was told that it was essential to speak honestly about myself, my alcohol addiction, and my relationship with my family and friends. This was painfully embarrassing to me. I believed the group wouldn't understand my plight. In addition, I was appalled by the tragic stories the other group members told. I knew that a similar type of outpouring was expected of me, but I vowed to myself, "There is no way that I'm going to let these people know how terrible I am." Even though the thought of disclosing my secrets frightened me, I saw the immense relief my fellow group members felt after telling about their painful lives and emotions.

As my trust for my counselor and my group grew, I was able to risk being honest with them. Even so, it was very hard to do. But it was such a relief not to run away from myself and others any longer. At first, I shared some minor hidden incidents, carefully watching the reaction of the group.

One thing I divulged was, "I really drank more than the two drinks a day I first admitted to." It surprised me that no one in the group was shocked in the least. So I decided to test them with another secret like, "My husband and I used to fight every time I would drink." Again there was no disbelief in their faces. It was as if I was telling their story by telling my story.

No matter what I said, my group members listened to me. They offered me support and gave me encouragement, and they didn't laugh at me or ridicule me for creating so much havoc in my life. No one said, "You are a bad person and a failure." Instead, they accepted and loved me for myself. Nor did they judge or berate me for my past mistakes. This was something I had never encountered before. It was wonderful. At last I didn't have to pretend any longer that I was someone else. I could be me. And, best of all, they actually liked me for myself. Never had I been so totally honest about myself and yet received so much love in return. Like each of the others, never had I felt such relief and peace.

Once I started to open up, years of anguish began to unlock. Even though it took a very long time to unravel the tangled web of stored emotions, I found it was a necessary process if I desired to free myself from the bonds of this disease called alcoholism.

By identifying with other people in the group, I was able to gain many personal insights. I could tell Eric in group, "I know how you feel; I have experienced the same feelings." When I recognized myself and my actions in others, it helped me to see my total self far more clearly. The observations of my new friends enabled me to identify specific characteristics and behaviors that I couldn't see before. When Helena said to me, "It sounds like you used alcohol to run away from yourself," it was like a light had been turned on inside of me.

After a few moments I replied, "It's true. I always felt worthless. But then I found alcohol and it made me feel better about myself."

Accepting new communication skills continued to be a vital challenge. I had gone through life with minimal knowledge about communication. All my life I believed that no one would be interested in my thoughts or feelings, so I generally wouldn't discuss anything, let alone share personal matters. When I drank, vocalizing was much easier. Now that I was in treatment, I was informed by my counselor, Sam, "You need to learn how to communicate, and without chemicals." Even though this sounded like a simple goal, it was very demanding, since my shyness and insecurity continuously held me back. Although I attempted to open myself to my group and other patients, hoping to be accepted despite my faults, my fear of rejection still frequently blocked the way.

I could see that changing my communication patterns wasn't going to happen overnight. Communicating with other people was not just a matter of verbalizing my thoughts and feelings. Another idea I was given in treatment was that the most significant element in effective communication is listening. I was taught in group to ask myself, "How well do I listen? Am I really listening, or am I thinking about something else, or am I considering how I'm going to respond?" I had never before thought about the different methods of communication. One day in group Sam suggested that I examine this area more closely and attempt to identify the communication patterns of my family and friends.

The first person who came to mind was my friend Jenifer. I told the group that she continually had operated on the assumption that what she said was far more important than what others offered. I could almost hear her mind racing ahead, preparing the next statement rather than listening to what I was saying. Her vacant stare, along with some non-committal response, told me that her thoughts were preoccupied and she didn't hear anything I said. Not only was it frustrating to attempt to converse with Jenifer, but it hurt me far more than I was willing to admit. Because of my own self-doubts, our interactions intimidated me. Often I withdrew in frustration and said to myself, "What's the use?"

Waiting for group to start one day, I was glancing over the column of communication styles listed in the group room and I recognized a style that reminded me of my parents. My mother, Betty, tended to do all of the talking in our family. My father, Leonard, withdrew into himself. So often she spoke for my dad, since he refused to be involved in family interactions. Yet he wouldn't tell her that he resented this. Instead, he suppressed his feelings and when he had reached a certain limit, he told her to shut up, or got even in some way.

I had thought that their one-sided conversations was the way to communicate. My parents had no equality while relating to one another, no listening or interest, but only toleration of each other.

When group started I told the group about my parent's communication patterns. I suddenly realized that my mother had used talking as a defense in order to avoid dealing with her feelings. Silence made her uncomfortable, so she spent time talking about anything that came to mind. Following a monologue by my mother was very hard and I often lost my concentration. What she didn't realize was that when she explained too much, she took the chance of others misunderstanding what she wanted to communicate.

I remember another painful lesson about communication and trust that happened some years ago. Even though my friend Kara tended to talk about herself constantly, to others she appeared to be a sweet and caring person. I often overlooked her manipulation and desire for individual gratification. One time we were on a committee and she wanted to be in charge of an entire project, but planned to eliminate parts that she felt were unnecessary, particularly one segment that I was involved in. Other members told me she had become quite friendly with the organization's president, undermining my accomplishments. However, I didn't want to believe that my friend would do anything to hurt me. Then one day I told her what I had heard and asked if it was true. Though she denied any wrongdoing immediately, and tried to change the subject, her face and body announced her guilt. Her face flushed red and she stammered, couldn't look at me directly, and squirmed uncomfortably in her chair.

Several days later at a meeting, the president indirectly disclosed that my fears were well-founded. With my trust shattered, I became disheartened and hurt. I decided that I didn't want her friendship or to be used any longer. For me it was an extremely sad and painful lesson of dishonest communication.

As I further examined communication patterns, I seriously looked at the unhealthy dialogue habits that my husband and I had. In my drinking days, communication with John usually ended up in an argument. When intoxicated, my self-image was at its lowest point, so I over-reacted to anything that appeared to be criticism. If he said at dinner, "I don't care for this casserole," I would become defensive and say, "You don't like anything I cook," and go off in a huff. No matter how insignificant a comment might be, I blew it out of proportion. I used those disagreements as justification to drink. Then, after awhile, I purposely started an argument so that I had a legitimate excuse to drink. However, if anyone had confronted me with this manipulative practice, I would have denied it vigorously.

Another area I had problems with, particularly when I had been drinking, was frequently misinterpreting what another person said. If I felt insecure and I thought the person was negative toward me, I reacted in a defensive manner. Since I had misunderstood the meaning of the message, the communication was lost.

As I continued to examine my communication patterns, I saw another one that fit me. One of the habits I had previously developed was assuming that I knew what another person was thinking or feeling. Yet I didn't always check it out with that person. I learned in group that it was necessary to constantly remind myself that I was not inside of the other person, that it was impossible to really know what another person was experiencing. Naturally, I was sometimes wrong in interpreting another person's feelings. Yet, because of my own insecurities, I often believed others were thinking badly of me. The reality probably was that they had matters other than me on their minds.

Too often I believed I was communicating with others when I was just mouthing empty words. However, each time I didn't explain my thoughts and feelings thoroughly, my group let me know immediately. My counselor explained, "Listening to another person's tone of voice helps identify hidden feelings that are difficult to express." So often, especially when I was drinking, I had trouble listening.

After I had been in treatment for several weeks, my friend Arthur came to visit me. He made a lengthy explanation to me regarding a personal problem he was having with his wife, Marion. Even though I cared about both of them, I wasn't completely listening and found myself gazing around the room, tapping my foot, and fidgeting. Of course, he sensed my impatience and became flustered, losing his train of thought completely. Even though I apologized, saying, "I'm sorry," a momentary barrier came between us. Suddenly I remembered Sam's lecture in group about body language. He had told the group, "Body language sometimes says far more than words can ever convey. It communicates inner feelings, even when we're not even aware of them." I realized that I needed to be more attentive to the messages my body was giving. I uncrossed my legs and arms, leaned forward, and looked Arthur in the eyes. "Go on," I said, "I'm interested in what happened next." Like magic, the barrier between us dissolved and my friend finished telling me a matter of great concern to him—and I counted one more personal victory.

Since learning in treatment to use direct eye contact and observe facial expressions, I was able to establish better communication. In the evenings during visiting hours, I concentrated on practicing my new skills with my husband. During the process, I noticed that John, like Arthur, really liked it when I gave him my undivided attention. It let him know I was interested in *him*, as well as in what he said.

Since I wanted to grow into a healthy human being, I needed to understand and accept both the unpleasant as well as the pleasant components of my complete self. When I took away all of the camouflage that I protected myself with—the lies, the distortions, and the fantasies—it was scary to be exposed. But I found there was personal acceptance and love waiting for me, for what I was and not for some phony image that I tried unsuccessfully to portray to others. As I discovered new things about myself and found answers concerning my life, I also took a new interest in other people and how they solved problems. I really cared about my friends and what happened to them. If I could assist them in any way, I would do so.

Along with group therapy and lectures, part of the treatment program included what is called Family Week. Family Week consisted of each patient's family members attending educational lectures and group sessions at the treatment center for five days during the patient's stay. They learned about co-dependency traits, control issues, and communication skills. They also spent time together identifying how they had been affected by the disease. Family members could talk about their bitter emotions regarding the patient's behavior. Even though it was a painful period for our family, this week was a real turning point for all of us. Just prior to Family Week I experienced a great deal of apprehension. The truth was, I had a dim hope that maybe my counselor would tell me that my family didn't need to be present that week.

After all, I told Counselor Sam, "I'm doing so well that it certainly isn't necessary for them to come." Downright terror was really underneath my surface apprehension. I was worried about what my family would say about me and fearful that they wouldn't want me back, especially if I talked about my true feelings with them. When my daughter Lorene continually expressed on the phone, "Mom, I just can't wait for Family Week to arrive," my panic grew.

Throughout treatment, patients participated in each group member's Family Week. We observed and gave feedback to at least six other families regarding their interactions with each other. After participating in several Family Weeks, I was emotionally wrung out. As I watched various hurting families explore their pain, I could see what was before me. Being in the "hot seat" (the term used for a patient's Family Week) was not something I looked forward to. I prayed, "Please let me die and go to heaven. After all," I reminded my Creator, "I have already suffered a great deal and I'm truly sorry for my behavior." But as Family Week approached, it was apparent that God had other plans for me and didn't agree with my desperate proposal.

During the first few days of Family Week, my children and husband shared a fraction of their pain, along with their perception of my behavior, in the group therapy sessions. Of course, I had already told my group a different version of my life. So when my family mentioned something contrary to my description, I was quick to defend and offer the "correct" version. When John told me, "I never knew what shape you would be in when I came home from work," my defenses went up immediately. Then Renae informed me, "I was so scared when you and Daddy fought every day.

I would hide in my room with my head under the pillow so I wouldn't hear anything." Completely embarrassed, I thought, "What will my new friends think of me?" So of course I clarified her statement instantly, saying, "We didn't fight every day, just once in awhile."

While I protected myself from the testimonies with contradictions, one obstacle lay before me. My counselor. There was no way that Sam would let me get away with this tactic (he was becoming a real pain). Instead, he informed me that I was in "denial" again. Denial was a nagging word that seemed to follow me wherever I went, continually blocking my progress in recovery.

With a wounded expression on my face, I shut up and began to listen. And what I heard was pure pain. It shook me to my soul. I started to realize how much agony my children and my husband had gone through. How could I have been so blind? I began to see how each one of us had been affected by this all-consuming disease. At long last, my eyes were finally opening. I couldn't medicate myself anymore, so I was forced to honestly look at the devastation of my life. This ugly picture was not at all what I had wanted for our family life when John and I were first married. It was extremely hard for me to accept how this disease of addiction had destroyed our family.

A new revelation was that my husband had used his work as an escape during my drinking years. John was unable to deal with my increased drinking or my unstable behavior, so he tried to avoid his misery by working hard. It was the only place he was safe from my negative and unforgiving attitude.

Speaking ever more freely, John told the group, "The pressures of parenting and being a husband were often overwhelming, so my work became my refuge, the only place that I felt secure." To add to the problem, as the years passed and my drinking escalated, his self-image suffered. He told me, "I felt helpless that I couldn't stop your drinking. By spending more hours developing a successful business, I gained the self-confidence that I didn't experience at home." As he poured out more and more of himself, my defenses crumbled.

But it wasn't until I was in treatment that we saw how his work had become a preoccupation for John. Realizing that he, too, was developing symptoms of the disease was not easy for him to accept. He became aware that he had to deal with his own compulsion to work, just as I had to come to grips with my addiction to alcohol.

John loved our children very much, yet at times he admitted that he had difficulty relating to them on a personal level. He felt unable to talk to them about his growing concerns regarding my drinking, or about their own disruptive behaviors, which he was seeing develop in them.

During my drinking years, John and I actually lived separate lives, although we resided in the same home. "There were even times," John said, "when I wished you would die, freeing me from our miserable marriage." Whenever he experienced thoughts of this nature he said, "I felt so guilty."

In a way, John said he experienced a sense of reassurance when he learned about the symptoms of the disease of addiction. Even though he definitely didn't like what had happened to him in our dysfunctional family system, it was a relief to know that he was not losing his mind.

When we look back to an incident following Family Week, we now know how much a part of the disease he was. Once Family Week was completed, I was entitled to go on a weekend pass. As a reward for ourselves, John and I decided to go shopping. However, I didn't end up buying anything, but John did. He found this incredible bargain (I know it's hard to believe)—a red, white and blue plaid suit. Even though I had some reservations about the suit, John liked it enough to buy it.

Today, we laugh about it. John readily admits, "You know, I must have been pretty sick to have had such terrible judgment. I can't believe I bought such a hideous suit." As a reminder, I saved the suit; it makes a great Halloween costume.

So the healing process began. We stopped blaming each other, took responsibility for our personal behavior, and moved into recovery. It was critical for John and me to concentrate on our individual healing and not be tempted to direct the healing of the other. John admitted, "I brought you to treatment to get fixed up, but now I see that I have a few things to fix myself."

It was apparent that our family had only touched the surface of our pain. We knew there was a lot of work yet to be done, but it was a start, and that was the key. The recovery of our family hinged on the acceptance of our family disease, as well as being honest and willing to change our lives. The areas that our family needed to examine were many. Dealing with one problem at a time was slow and, in time, all the past must be dealt with. When that happened, Sam promised, we would all be completely free at last.

With each small step, we removed our barriers and worked through the emotional pain. As our pain dwindled, it allowed our tentative love and trust to emerge and little by little grow stronger. By sharing our feelings and accepting each other, faults and all, John and I have now learned what true recovery is really about.

After discarding each remnant of pain, I couldn't believe how much better I felt, how light and free and full of inner calmness. The heaviness in my heart and soul had slowly disappeared.

Unquestionably there have been and will be alarming setbacks. Some people call these "failures," but I now re-frame failure to mean only a setback. If my goal is to grow emotionally and become a healthy, productive, honest human being, it is critical not to allow the setbacks in life to deter me from this primary goal. I need to keep in mind that I have inner strengths that I am not always aware of.

I owe a tremendous debt to my counselor, Sam, and my group members, for without their honesty and caring I wouldn't be here today. At times I fought them. Other times I hated them because they could see through my walls into my soul. So often this process of putting my life back together was agonizingly painful. There were moments when I thought I was falling apart, but their love and caring saw me through the pain. It seemed like I shed buckets of tears and used boxes of tissues. At that time, I suspected the treatment center must have stock in the tissue company, since there were always so many boxes of them in the group rooms. If they didn't, they certainly missed a great opportunity for subsidizing treatment.

Whenever I think back on our family's recovery path, I find it hard to believe that through so many years I didn't see that my life had become unmanageable. Often I asked myself, "How could I have ignored the obvious signs, wasting our precious lives so carelessly?" The insanity of this disease of addiction and its system of denial never ceases to amaze me.

Even though in the beginning my consent to go to treatment was primarily because of my family's insistence, deep inside me I didn't want to lose them. During treatment my family and I were able to deal with many obstacles in our lives. It was a wonderful relief to finally take the blinders off and to take responsibility for my choices, no matter how misguided they were. The doors of communication were opened for John and me as we attempted to repair the misery and destruction in our marriage. There was no question that we were both fearful of the future and what it might hold for us. So many serious mistakes had been made, so much suffering had been a part of our lives for such a long time. However, we made a commitment to ourselves and each other to both work at rebuilding our lives and our marriage.

Near the end of treatment, our twenty-second wedding anniversary occurred. John and I had invested a lot of time together, whether happy or miserable. We also had three beautiful children whom we both loved very much. Still, the decision to dedicate ourselves to a full-time recovery plan was not an easy one. Nevertheless, we vowed to give ourselves some time and to do our best to save our marriage and our family. We hoped it wouldn't take twenty-two years to restore our marriage, but we could work on it each day.

However, this was easier to say than to practice. While I was in treatment, John often had dinner with me at the Center. In order to find some privacy and work off our dinner, we were allowed to take walks around the block. On one of our strolls following Family Week, I became very quiet. With so many emotions whirling around in my mind, I was confused about their meaning. Sensing something was wrong, John persistently asked what was troubling me. My first impulse was to shout at him, "Leave me alone!" The more he questioned me, the further I withdrew. Yet he was determined to break through my wall.

Then, without warning, tears began flowing down my face. Taken by surprise, John reached out and gently put his arm around my shoulders. Quietly he asked me again what was bothering me. I told him how frightened I was of all of my exposed feelings and how to handle them. Going on, I explained, as well as I could between sobs, that I felt like a newborn baby, defenseless and uncertain about what I was to do with my life. I told him, "I'm so scared that I'll mess up our lives again." Then John became silent. Stopping on the sidewalk, he turned me toward him. Looking down into my eyes he said, "I'm scared about our future, too."

4

BEGINNINGS

Now and then memories of a small child lying in bed at
night, crying silently in emotional pain, have come back to
me. Those recollections always surface at unexpected moments, yet when I feel my suppressed tears break loose, it
gives me some release. Why I cry I'm not certain, but I feel
so lonely and sad when I wake up, completely bewildered.
When this happened in the old days, there was no one for
me to turn to or talk to about the growing fears and
insecurities that were taking control of me.

After my first few weeks in treatment, past silenced
memories began to surface. Of course, during treatment I
had no alcohol to block my recollections, so they were free
to emerge at any time. Although it was threatening, my
counselor reassured me that it was time to look at those
shadowed areas of my life.

One vision, whether a suppressed memory or just a
dream, I'm not certain, returned to haunt me many times.
It was a scene that pictured me trying to run down a winding
path from something that wasn't visible. Sometimes the day
was sunny, other times it was rainy, and often it was completely dark. I was clothed only in my slip, and try as I might,

my limbs felt as though heavy arm and leg weights restrained them. In my slow motion flight of terror, my heart pounded so fast that I thought it would burst into a thousand pieces. Then suddenly I'd awaken in a panic, instantly followed by exhaustion and intense relief. It was only a dream.

Although no clear answers have clarified the meaning of the dream, I suspect something frightening occurred which triggered my nightmare. Some day, when the time is right, I know that the explanation will be revealed to me. Even so, I'm apprehensive about the unknown.

While recalling my dream I looked back at other events in my childhood, allowing long forgotten memories to surface. Many of them had to do with the pain surrounding love. A particularly bitter experience happened when I was about four years old. Since my family was moving from one town to another, we left our cocker spaniel, Sport, with my uncle Jake while we checked out our new home. It was my understanding that we would pick up my dog when we returned, so on our journey home my excitement about soon seeing Sport grew steadily.

Shortly after we arrived at my uncle's home, I found out that he had given our dog away. I was completely devastated. I cried out, "How could you do this to me?" I felt totally deceived and heartbroken at the news. If my uncle loved me, why would he give away our precious dog, whom I loved so much? Uncle Jake responded, "Honey, I'm so sorry, but I thought you knew there was no room for Sport at your new home." Suddenly, I realized that my parents must have known he was going to discard my friend. Bewildered and in pain, I questioned them, "If I can't trust my parents and my uncle, who can I trust? Didn't you all know how much I loved Sport?" Ignoring my emotional display, my parents turned away. Confused, there was absolutely no way I could understand why they had done such a terrible thing. Sometimes I wondered if it was because of me that they gave Sport away. Maybe I hadn't taken care of him as well as I could have. Whenever I broke into tears of sadness, my parents told me, "Stop being such a baby; it's only a dog." So I tried to suppress my feelings and pretend that it didn't hurt so much. It took a long time for me to get over the loneliness and grief at losing my companion, and I never got over the betrayal.

As a child I learned to denounce my feelings as not being real, so it isn't surprising that I unconsciously decided to ignore them and pretend they didn't exist. When I was told by my parents that I was "bad" to feel angry, I felt guilty about my anger. Feeling guilty then became another part of my distorted personal belief system. It is no wonder that I believed I had no right to my feelings. Growing up with these damaging messages certainly inhibited my emotional stability and development. So it follows that when I entered adulthood I chastised myself with, "You shouldn't feel that way," or "Nice little girls don't show anger," or "Big girls aren't afraid."

While I was in treatment, I also learned that honest communication, openness, and positive images are established in what is called a "functional family system." However, I knew none of these characteristics fit the family model that I came from. One of my treatment assignments was to examine my unfamiliar family background. It was a difficult project, since I was cautious about probing into this vast and often blank area. I asked myself, "Was mine a family that had meaningful communication? Was it a family where we were open and honest with each other, while reinforcing positive self-images?" My immediate response was "no" to each question.

Those questions brought back memories of a time when I was about five and I had both of my arms accidentally pulled out of the shoulder sockets. Within a few weeks time, my cousin Kevin yanked out one arm and my brother Jack dislocated the other arm. It was so terribly painful that I couldn't quit crying. My mother tried to stop my tears by telling me, "It doesn't hurt and, besides, big girls don't cry." Both of my arms were in slings to protect them from further injury. Added to my pain was the futility of not being able to do anything without help. Someone had to feed me and I couldn't dress myself or go to the bathroom without assistance. Whenever I cried in pain or frustration at my helplessness, I was reminded by my parents that crying wasn't acceptable. To this day, whenever I hear a parent say these words to a child, I want to scream, "Stop! Your child has a right to feelings!"

This was one of many incidents that contributed to my early lesson in denying both physical and emotional pain. I carried this powerful lesson throughout a good deal of my life. There are times when I slip back and think to myself, "Smile when you are afraid. Don't be honest or talk about your feelings. Deny yourself. Smile so people won't know you hurt. Never show anger or shame; smile instead." When this happens, I have to remind myself that these thoughts are unhealthy and destructive to my self-worth.

Feelings of insecurity, worthlessness, and self-doubt evolved from my earliest childhood until some years after my treatment. Even though I'm unable to recall many specific events that affected my life positively or negatively, I've learned it isn't crucial to remember *everything*. On the other hand, it *is* critical to deal with my suppressed memories immediately after they come back to me. Realizing that I have the power to change the effects of my lonely life whenever I can has made a big difference in my recovery. I try not to dwell on what might have been.

In treatment I was told that it is important to determine what was truth and what was fantasy in the recollections of my childhood. One vivid incident happened when I was about six while on a camping trip in the mountains with my family. After we had set up camp, my parents, my older brother and sister, and I were standing by the car.

Without warning there was a loud, screeching, whistling sound from across the field. Terrified of the noise, I scrambled under the car to hide from this terrible thing that was descending upon us. As I laid between the car wheels, trembling with fear, I could hear everyone laughing. Then my dad pulled me from under the car and chastised me for being a "baby." He said in a condescending voice, "I can't believe that you're afraid of a *train.*" The rest of the family continued to laugh and make fun of me. It hurt so much and I felt so stupid not to have recognized the sound of an approaching train. I didn't think that my family cared about me, or my feelings, so I stuffed my pain inside. The circumstances were definitely real, just as my emotional pain and humiliation were real. However, in order to minimize my suffering, I fantasized in my mind about different situations where I was always brave and strong, never afraid of anything. In that way I could hide from my shame in whatever fantasy I chose.

Throughout treatment, answers to my questions concerning my family system began to fall into place. It became clear that I grew up in a system of fear, afraid of my feelings, afraid to talk openly with family or friends and afraid to be myself. I was constantly afraid of receiving negative reactions because I didn't do things "right." When I did do well, I was afraid I'd receive no recognition for my accomplishments. It was a lifestyle that did little to promote healthy image-building for me. There was no doubt in my mind that the environment in which I grew up was referred to in the treatment jargon as a "dysfunctional family."

As I thought more and more about my childhood, trying to sort through the fragments of my jumbled history, another memory materialized. It happened when I was about age seven, after I fell down and hurt myself on our neighbor's graveled driveway. I had been told by my mom not to cry, but to "be strong" and be "a big girl." Nevertheless, the pain in my bloody, scratched knee was so severe that I was unable to keep from crying. In my mind were implanted the words, "If you are strong and don't cry, you will be a big girl." Therefore, if I cried, I must be the opposite of strong, which is weak. The inference that weak people are not acceptable was my interpretation—and that I was a weak person,

When our family went to church each Sunday morning, my older brother Jack, sister Pat, and I were expected to sit quietly throughout the service. The uncomfortable church pews were so hard that it was difficult for me to sit still, since I was quite thin and didn't have much padding on my posterior. Every time I changed position, I received a stern look from my dad, and my mom told me, "Control yourself." Not only was I a "weak" person, but I was someone who "couldn't control herself" either. Then I became angry at myself when I cried or fidgeted, repeating those same words to myself.

As an adult in recovery, it was now high time to question my childhood methods of dealing with my feelings. As I asked myself, "Did I stuff feelings inside or pretend they didn't exist? Did I act out my hurt and anger?" The answers came up "yes." I could finally see that all of those unhealthy patterns had been a part of my life since the beginning. In order to run away from my feelings because the pain was growing so great, I dreamed and pretended I was anyone other than myself. I frequently fantasized that I was a famous and talented celebrity who could cope with anything.

Searching further, I remembered that as a child I wanted a voice like the famous singer, Doris Day. Time after time I attempted to sing like her. The pitiful sounds that came out of my mouth did not even come close to resembling her lovely voice. Try as I might, I found that it didn't work when I attempted to make someone else's talents my own. Even with that information, I didn't stop trying. Many times I tried to imitate others, but in the end I became frustrated and disappointed because I wasn't successful.

Since I was always so shy, I had trouble making friends easily. It was particularly hard for me when I was in the second grade. That year our family moved to four different locations, where I attended four new schools. Each time we moved, I closed myself up more. I was afraid to make new friends, since I would have to leave them. After our last relocation, it was months before I allowed myself to make new friendships.

As a child I was very lonely, unassertive, and insecure. I felt completely inadequate, so it is no wonder that I became a lonely, unassertive, insecure adult. If anyone commended me for my triumphs, I immediately discounted myself and my achievements. I remember that when I was about twelve, I completed a pencil drawing of a mountain lake and surrounding trees for a school assignment. My teacher praised me for doing a great job, but I didn't accept her approval. Instead, I pointed out my mistakes. Feeling unworthy of positive acknowledgement was a normal response for me, so whenever any compliment was given, I was embarrassed by the attention. My self-image was so low that I sincerely believed I didn't deserve any honors. Most of the time I discarded the recognition, then changed the focus by talking about something else.

In my family, neither personal matters nor world situations were openly discussed. I knew nothing about politics, sports, or social customs. The phrase "Children are seen and not heard" was a common one my parents used to keep me in line any time I questioned their regulations. I was completely ignorant about the functions of men and women, so when I had my first menstrual period I had no idea what was happening. Terrified, I ran to my mom, crying because I thought I was bleeding to death. Embarrassed to talk about it, my mom closed her blue eyes and gave me a brief explanation that I didn't understand, then quickly changed the subject. Still confused and afraid, I went to the library, where no one knew me, for detailed information. After learning more about the normal process of monthly periods, I was somewhat relieved. Even so, the distinctive physical and emotional changes that were occurring in my body were bewildering to me. Typically, the matter was never discussed again by either my mom or me.

To add to my problems, I was confused about where I fit in, which path I was to take in life, and where I belonged. Even though I was on the verge of becoming an adult, I was constantly reminded by my parents that I was a child.

Whenever I tried to express myself about the current projects I was involved in at school, my parents changed the subject. If I attempted to talk about something they were uncomfortable with, they found an excuse to leave the room. Making mistakes or forgetting obligations wasn't tolerated. I recall one time when I was thirteen, I arranged to meet my friend, Alice, at four p.m., but she was very late. While I was waiting, my mind kept flashing to some responsibilities I was neglecting. I knew my parents would be upset with me if I didn't get my chores done. My frustration at being kept waiting was mounting and I was to the point of being angry. Then I thought, "Maybe Alice had an accident," so my guilty feelings surfaced and combined with the angry ones. Following that was some anxious concern, along with increasing worry. By now I was doubting myself. Maybe I hadn't made it clear regarding the time or place. It was true we had talked about several potential meeting places. Joining my other stored feelings was growing confusion.

Finally, after forty-five minutes, Alice arrived. She said, "Sorry I'm late; my mother's car had a flat tire." Throughout Alice's explanation, my irritation and anger were simmering inside of me. Rather than be honest and tell her what I was feeling I said, "Oh, that's okay." She had enough perception to notice that my voice tone didn't match my words. While I reassured Alice that I was fine, I completely ignored my suppressed feelings.

At that time in my life, I didn't know it wasn't okay—it isn't healthy—to leave my disregarded feelings suppressed inside, creating internal pressures. I certainly didn't want Alice to know that I was angry, worried, frustrated, confused, and relieved. After all, what would she think of me? Of course, she would assume that I am weak, inferior, and unable to keep control of my emotions. At all costs I believed I mustn't let anyone see the unpleasant side of me. Then my negative self-criticism started again.

When I got home, my mom was furious with me for being late, ignoring my explanation. When she told me, "Your dad will take care of you when he gets home," my fear intensified. After my dad arrived from work, I tried to tell him what happened, but he wouldn't listen either; he angrily wondered when I was going to grow up and be responsible. The only thing he was worried about was the fact that I didn't get the yard mowed and raked. As always, I knew some punishment would follow my dad's tirade. Shamed, I hung my head and accepted my penance of extra duties without comment.

For awhile, I thought I would be safe from hurt by isolating myself from involvement with friends. In that way I wouldn't get in trouble with my parents. Eventually I found out this wasn't the answer; it only increased my loneliness. Adding to the burden, I couldn't tell my friends how miserable I was at home, because I was too embarrassed. Sometimes it was too much trouble, as well as emotionally painful, to pretend that I felt good about myself in their company. More specifically, the risk was too great that others would eventually know how much I hated myself and find out my secret that "I am no good."

There was an incident that further affected my poor self-image when I was in the 8th grade. Wearing my new pink sweater and black skirt, I went to my first dance at the YMCA with my best friend Joan. Attending the function were boys and girls from various schools in our community.

Among them was a tall, handsome, popular boy, who had a group of friends constantly around him. He seemed to be well-liked and charming to everyone. For several hours I contemplated asking him to dance when there was a "girl's choice" dance. But each time one came up, I couldn't initiate enough courage.

Eventually, since the evening was about over, I cautiously approached him and said, "Would you like to dance with me?" He looked down at me with his amazing blue eyes looking directly into mine and said without hesitation, "I'm sorry, I can't; I have a broken leg." Completely believing his words, I responded naively, "Oh, I'm so sorry," and walked away. It wasn't until I was across the room that I realized what had just happened.

Not only was I embarrassed, but completely crushed. My already low self-image disintegrated when I realized the magnitude of ultimate rejection. This humiliating experience hurt me deeply, enabling me to build my protective walls around me even higher. And, as a result, it was several years before I attempted to ask a boy to dance again.

Looking back, it is heart-breaking that I gave so much power to the words people said to me. The lower my self-concept was, the more authority I gave to their words. My inferior image, that I wasn't okay and that I was unlovable, had just been validated by this young boy. I assumed that somehow he could tell that "I was a rotten person." Yet if someone would have asked me what was wrong, I would have denied my insecurities as well as my pain. A pattern that I had mastered in my dysfunctional family was to carry on, to pretend my life was all right. I had learned to "stuff" all of my feelings, even the joyful ones, down into the black hole of my heart.

Since I had come to believe that I was "bad," I also believed that no one can love a "bad" person. So that must be why my parents couldn't tell me they loved me. Each time someone implied anything that sounded the least bit critical, I told myself that, since I am "no good," the message must be true. I didn't know how to handle any kind of rejection without becoming self-critical. Whenever I chastised myself with cynical messages for being imperfect, my personal hate increased.

During my childhood, I had no understanding regarding the validity of my feelings. In my family, I learned early on that I was unprotected when I expressed how I felt inside. Whenever I did express emotions, particularly anger, I was punished with isolation in my room, critical put-downs, or denial of privileges. After awhile, I was so far away from my feelings that I didn't know what I felt anymore. Little did I know that when I closed myself down emotionally, I shut myself away, keeping others from becoming close to me. Not only did I isolate myself from feeling, but I protected myself from meaningful involvement with others.

Since my parents minimized my successes and looked primarily at my shortcomings, when I made a mistake, throughout my life I made it into a catastrophe. I magnified the incident totally out of proportion. Whenever I accomplished anything, I consistently put the event down and concentrated on the weaknesses in my performance. A particularly painful example was my first piano recital, when I was a freshman in high school. As I stood in the stage wings, nervously waiting for my debut, I was all but paralyzed with fear. My yellow print dress was clinging to my perspiring body and I just knew the audience would notice. More than anything I wanted to do well so my parents would be proud of me. When my turn came, numb with fear, I stumbled over my feet onto the stage. Somehow I made it to the piano bench, sat down, and began to play. The result was disastrous. Immediately my mind went blank and my fingers stiffened. After what seemed like an eternity, I reached the end of my piece. Quickly I ran off the stage, completely disgraced by my performance. I wanted to disappear from the world, away from the critical eyes watching me.

Although my teacher and other students tried to comfort me, I knew I had let my parents down. After the recital, my dad was waiting at the end of the hall, but he didn't look at me with his piercing brown eyes or say anything. Hidden behind his mustache were his tightly shut lips and stern face. Quickly he grabbed my arm, escorting me through the side door of the gym, away from any contact with friends. I knew he was upset and embarrassed. As he hurried me to the car, I could sense his shame and anger, but he wouldn't tell me what he was feeling or talk to me about my performance. Instead, he acted as if I wasn't alive. Crushed in spirit, wanting him to hold me and tell me it was okay, I cowered silently next to the car door as my dad drove home. There was no use in telling him how I felt; he wouldn't understand. Again I stuffed my feelings far inside. Trying to hold my tears back, I vowed never to perform again. The next day the family went about their business and nothing was ever said about that night again.

There were few times when I felt good inside about myself and my small successes. In high school, when I became a cheerleader, I believed I had something to offer. The students apparently liked me enough to vote for me to lead them in cheers. And the time I was elected to be a class officer became a great morale booster. When I was chosen as president of the Pep Club, I felt extremely honored. Then again, I experienced tremendous frustration along with a great deal of emotional anxiety each time I was less successful. If I didn't get a good grade on a test or my report card, I chastised myself, focusing on my stupidity. Also the fear of my dad's displeasure kept me from showing him the report card for days after receiving it. Even when I worked hard at school and brought home high grades, I never received praise from my parents.

Trying to please my dad rather than trying to please me eventually became an obsession with me. I came to believe that if I worked harder he would give me what I wanted—his acceptance, his love. Often I prayed to hear the words from him, "Joann, you did a great job and I'm proud of you," but it never happened. The harder I tried, the more frustrated I became. The only times he noticed me was when I did something wrong, such as not cleaning my room or not sweeping the floor of his barbershop. For years I pretended his disregard of me didn't matter, but now I realized it grieved me more than I admitted.

A critical turning point for me came following a painful incident that happened shortly after my fifteenth birthday. Even though I had obtained my driver's permit, my parents hadn't encouraged me to drive, so my sweetheart, John, offered to teach me in his car. After several weeks of driving practice, I wanted to show off for my dad. One Sunday, with some persuasion, he let me drive the family car to his barbershop to do some cleaning. As I got behind the wheel of our light blue sedan, my hands began to shake and my heart beat fast. Suddenly my confidence disappeared and fear completely took over. Immediately after leaving our driveway, I made mistake after mistake, crossing the center line, jerking to a stop, and forgetting to signal. My dad was upset with me, especially when I narrowly missed a parked car near the shop. Upon leaving, after cleaning the shop in silence, my dad drove home, refusing to acknowledge me or talk to me. For a long time I wasn't allowed to touch the car. Besides being hurt, my self-confidence was badly shaken, leaving me with nothing but guilt and shame about creating another disappointment for my parents.

Devastated, I wondered if there was anything I could do that would ever satisfy my dad or, for that matter, my mom. Since there was little or no approval for my accomplishments, I had finally figured out that striving to achieve was hardly worth the effort. No matter what I did, I always ended up living out my parents expectations of not being good enough in anything I attempted. The price of achievement just wasn't worth the pain, so I gave up. After my unfortunate driving episode, I discovered that giving up was far easier and less frustrating than attempting to achieve and then having a setback. The fear of receiving criticism gave me permission to give up even before I started, so I didn't have to suffer the humiliation of defeat.

When all of my life I believed "something is wrong with me," it's not surprising that I didn't feel like I fit in anywhere and was inferior to other people. Every time something was amiss in my life, I felt responsible for it, telling myself, "It must be my fault." If my parents fought, I thought it was my fault. Or if my parents argued about money, I believed it was because my mother spent too much on my clothes. With the "I can't do anything . . . I don't deserve anything" attitude, I eventually learned to become a victim. I fully expected my life to be miserable and for things to go wrong. And it came true.

Since I was consumed with my own pain, I didn't see that my parents showed their love in other ways. When I was growing up, they were generous in giving me possessions, such as clothes and paying for a piano and lessons, along with supplying my educational needs. Sewing was a pleasure my mother enjoyed, so she made various beautiful outfits for me during my school years.

Some years later, when I married and had children, my parents showed love by helping our family in countless ways. They assisted us in moving. They babysat on occasion. Whenever possible, they helped our family by purchasing basic household needs when our finances were insufficient. During my marriage, my dad showed his love by fixing objects needing repair. It gave him satisfaction to make things for our family and friends.

Mom and dad both came from similar rigid families where love, affection, and praise weren't expressed. And, because of this, both of my parents had difficulty in showing affection. However, my dad was the most rigid of the two. In his entire lifetime he never once told me in words that he loved me. Yet I desperately hoped in vain that someday he would express to me those cherished words, "I love you."

There is no question in my mind that my parents raised me in the best manner they were aware of, but it doesn't erase the years of loneliness and hurt. They didn't know that my life lacked the healthy living skills that I needed in order to cope with life successfully. They didn't realize that their constant discounting of my emotions eventually became part of my belief system. Since I was taught as a child that the expression of feelings, whether positive or negative, wasn't acceptable in any form, it was inevitable that, in any new relationship, my choices and responses would be affected by my beliefs. It wasn't until many years later did I see just how much my relationship with my husband and children was affected by what I learned as a child.

In any case, growing up in a dysfunctional home did not alone make me become an alcoholic, nor did my low self-esteem or not being able to express my feelings cause me to become dependent on alcohol. However, I believe that the combination of my low self-esteem, poor communication skills, the suppression of feelings, and the inability to deal with my feelings are all primary factors that assisted the development of my disease. In my case, when all of these elements were combined with the genetic predisposition, that is, not being able to process alcohol/drugs in my body, I was emotionally and physically set up to become an alcoholic, like dry tinder waiting for a match. All I needed was the deadly spark of alcohol to fan the flame of my disease.

5

SEARCH FOR LOVE

AFTER A FEW WEEKS IN TREATMENT, the group sessions were less threatening to me. In fact, I was beginning to look forward to them. Of course I wasn't going to let Sam know how much I enjoyed the group process. Since he liked my "Manipulation" paper, he just might think up another project for me. However, absolutely nothing got by Sam. His built-in radar, along with his x-ray eyes, gave him the power to know and see what was going to happen before anyone else did. One day in group, Sam innocently asked me, "Now that your suppressed memories are surfacing, how is that helping you?"

Feeling apprehensive, I responded meekly, "I feel much better, thank you," hoping he would move on to someone else.

Of course Sam wouldn't let it stop there. He continued probing, "Have you had any recent memories?"

I knew what was coming; he wasn't the only one with radar perception. Since treatment emphasized being honest about myself, it had made some impact on me. Sighing, I reluctantly said, "As a matter of fact, I have."

I knew what his next comment was going to be and Sam didn't disappoint my prediction. Persistently, he went on, "Why don't you tell the group about some of your memories and then they can let you know their impressions?"

It had happened once more, the funny-haired bugger had won, cleverly trapping me with my own revelations. Defeated, I told him, "Okay, if you insist." Taking a deep breath, I revealed to the group some recent thoughts that had been bothering me for a long time. When I was in the eighth grade, my parents felt that my best friend Joan wasn't a good influence for me. Since it was hard for me to make friends in the first place, I wasn't about to give up my friend as they requested. Without their knowledge, Joan and I went to movies, or met at the customary school hangout, and sometimes got together at school ball games. I didn't really like sneaking around behind my parent's backs, but it seemed the only way to keep our friendship alive.

Then one beautiful spring day, my shaky relationship with my parents erupted into physical violence. Earlier in the day, my friend Joan and I decided to skip school and go to the park, followed by a movie. We had a great time. To our misfortune, the teacher informed our parents about our absence at school that day. When I got home, my mother was furious. Following a very heated confrontation with my mom, accompanied by my persistent denial, our argument became physical. My mother slapped my face, telling me to stop lying, then hit my shoulders repeatedly while I was trying to fend her off. At that point, I was getting angry and afraid that I might hit my mom in return, so I ran out the door crying. Running as fast as I could, with tears blinding me, I wanted to get far away from my home.

My friend Tonia lived a few miles away, so, after running for several blocks, I decided to walk to her home. Feeling sorry for my plight, she gave me comfort and refuge. My plan was to run away permanently and go to California. I thought it was a wonderful way to punish my parents. While my friend and I were outside of her home discussing my options, the evening turned to darkness. Before I realized it, my parents were driving down the street. My dad was leaning out the car window yelling, "Joann, get into the car! Right now!"

Since I had always been afraid of my father's anger, my automatic response was to follow his orders. With a sense of defeat and my independent dreams now shattered, we all drove away in silence. As a consequence, the controls in my home were drastically tightened and I was grounded for several weeks. As with most situations, we never talked about the incident or the feelings seething beneath the surface. The usual way a problem was dealt with in our family was to ignore it and then pretend it didn't happen. Our family philosophy was, if we don't talk about it, then it's not an issue.

When I had finished my narrative, I touched my face and discovered that tears had been flowing down my cheeks. After some discussion and lots of support from my group, the pain began to subside. It had become apparent to me that my fear of my dad had controlled me most of my life. To our sad misfortune, we had missed out on so much.

Later that night, as I stretched out exhausted on my bed in the privacy of my room, my mind wouldn't rest. Reflecting on my adolescent years, I could see how emotionally vulnerable and immature I had been. My parents and I went through a constant power struggle that kept us from dealing effectively with conflict. It seemed like my parents were either trying to control me or I was trying to control them and somehow we missed meeting on common ground.

Naturally there were times when I wanted to make my own choices, but my parents saw my actions as complete disregard for their rules. I felt that they wanted to control my every move, as well as choose my clothes and pick my friends. Our power struggles became a battle of wills, with each of us trying to get our own way.

As I became older, I inherited more responsibility to complete certain chores around the house. Whenever it was my duty to vacuum the house, I dreaded it because in my heart I knew it wouldn't be good enough. Then there were the times when I helped my mother with the laundry. Although I tried, I never sorted and washed the clothes properly, according to my mother. So I thought it must be me, that I was the problem. I must be stupid not to do simple tasks correctly.

In an attempt to keep the reins tight, my parents over-disciplined me, and when I refused to "mind" they saw it as outright rebellion. On the other hand, I saw their persistent controlling as "treating me like a child." I fought against my parent's domination of my spirit, of my entire being, by what I interpreted as unrealistic demands. In order to get even, I neglected my household responsibilities or didn't clean up my messy room. Getting into trouble with my teachers at school was another way to rebel, as was defying my parents by coming home after curfew. I kept trying to convince myself, "I don't care anymore."

Living this up-and-down existence was like being on a speeding roller coaster with no place to get off. There were many highs, lows, and twisting turns in my life that created intense pressures for me, both internal and external. Struggling with myself, I wondered, "What kind of hopes can a 'nobody' like me have?" At other times, the knots of fear literally made me sick to my stomach.

It wasn't until I was in treatment that I could see that much of my guilt stemmed from my rebellious behavior toward my parents. Not only did I feel guilty about my actions, but I felt guilty about everything that went wrong in our family. Many nights, while lying in bed, I heard my parents arguing loudly about what to do about me. Feeling guilty, I questioned myself, "Maybe if I had been a better daughter, my parents wouldn't fight with each other or be mad at me." Any time these thoughts came, I quickly suppressed them, avoiding the hurt of never quite measuring up.

Although some of my friends were allowed to date during junior high, my parents felt that I was too young. Of course, I went to several parties at friends homes where boys were included, but this was not considered a date. As long as I was with a group, my parents didn't seem to object.

As I entered high school I was attracted to a couple of boys, but I was too shy to talk to them. I never forgot my experience of the rude boy's rejection at my first dance a couple of years before. However, during my freshman year, I was captivated by a handsome basketball player named John. He was over six feet tall, very good looking, and had dark hair and a smile that could melt ice cubes. Our first, exciting meeting occurred in the spring following a church function. Afterward, a number of friends were offered a ride, so we climbed into the back of a straw-filled pickup that belonged to one of John's classmates.

Our adventuresome driver decided to sneak the truck into our local drive-in movie theater. Everyone thought it was a great idea. He reasoned that if he backed in, anyone watching would think we were leaving. In any event, we weren't challenged, so we settled down to watch the movie. Throughout the evening I was distracted by the tall, handsome junior. To stir up interest, we flirted with each other by having a sword fight with pieces of straw. Since we had difficulty taking our eyes off one another, the movie, along with the other occupants of the truck, all went unnoticed for the rest of the evening.

During the next few weeks, every time I encountered John at school, my heart beat wildly and my breathing ceased. Glancing shyly toward each other, we said "Hi!" as we passed in the halls. Since he was an upperclassman, I was thrilled he even noticed me. Prom time was growing close and I hoped against hope that he would ask me to go. The inside word among my friends was that he would. One day, as we were passing in the hall, he actually said, "Would you like to go to the prom with me?" And as I continued walking down the hall, afraid to look at him, I timidly said "Yes," but loud enough that he could hear! That was all there was to our second romantic encounter, but it was enough to keep me dreaming about being together at the prom in a few weeks.

When prom day finally arrived, I was nervous and fearful that John wouldn't like me. Even though dancing was always fun for me, I feared I would step all over his feet when we danced. Finally the hour came when he stood at my front door holding a corsage in his hand. With my nerves tight, I tried to give the appearance of calmness. My knees were shaking under my new, full-length, pink brocade satin dress as John escorted me to his friend's car. Somehow I managed to maneuver my gown into the back seat without too much of a problem. I actually got it caught in the door only once. After greeting John's friend Bob, the driver, and his date, I tried to relax, breathe slowly, and stop babbling incoherently about nothing.

The dance was heavenly. I still remember the prom theme, "Stairway to the Stars," and how I felt complete ecstasy when I danced with "my" John. Throughout the evening I gazed admiringly at his handsome face and into his green eyes. As he tenderly held me in his arms, I knew I was in love. In that moment I was certain this wonderful person was for me, forever and ever plus two days. The term "forever and ever plus two days" became a love signature for both of us on cards and letters from then on.

At that time, there was one thing in particular that my parents did that drove me up the wall. John and I had gone together since the end of my freshman year. Whenever we came home from a date, we would sit in his car, talking about our future. Of course, some hugging and kissing went on as well. Approximately ten minutes after the car lights were turned off, the front porch light on my house would flick off and on. Following a ten-minute pause, the light would flicker again and again. After about the third time, I knew I was in trouble, so I tiptoed into the house. However, if I was angry at my parents for some reason, I punished them by staying another fifteen or twenty minutes in the car.

After I went into the house, neither of my parents were waiting at the door to confront me, nor were they even visible. True to the family code, nothing was said about it the next day by any of us, as though the incident never occurred. However, if there was a new pair of shoes or a particular sweater I wanted, I knew it would be denied me.

6

NUPTIAL DREAM

Even while I was still under the "protection and guidance" of my parents, I dreamed about the great things I would do with my life. Being a movie star, a champion ice skater, or a famous writer were my illusions of success. But, in my heart, I knew these visions wouldn't really happen. Besides being afraid of living, I was completely unprepared financially, emotionally, and socially to cope with most prospects of life on my own.

Since John and I had been going together for three years, I figured I was adult enough to at least handle marriage, family, and a meaningful relationship. Besides, I had been disillusioned at home for some time, so I knew that life would be much happier sharing it with the man I loved. Even though I experienced a certain amount of fear and anxiety as I searched for my independence, there was a special excitement concerning my journey into a new life.

John and I married following my graduation from high school. Even though the months of preparations were hectic, our wedding was very beautiful. Throughout high school we had been sweethearts, planning our July wedding for many months. Most of all, we were in love and full of hopes and dreams. At the same time, we didn't consider our youthfulness to be a disadvantage for a lifetime of happiness together. After all, I was all of eighteen and John was a charming older man of twenty.

With all the festivities of a formal wedding, everything was picture perfect—well, almost perfect. To start off, I arrived early at the church to dress, but just ten minutes before the ceremony I saw John driving away from the church in his car. Of course I had heard of brides being left at the altar, so I feared the worst. To my relief, about eight minutes later, he drove back into the parking lot. After the ceremony, I learned that John had forgotten my wedding ring at home. Even though I had seen situations like this in movies, I never dreamed this kind of thing would happen to me.

A short time later, with my nerves still on edge, the wedding march finally started. Taking a deep breath and with my dad to lean on, I willed my legs to move. Somehow I managed gracefully to walk down the aisle of our church in my beautiful, long white wedding dress and flowing veil. After I met my handsome John at the altar, I became calm inside. As we gazed lovingly at each other, our friend Father Thomas started the wedding service. Shortly after the ceremony began, I heard tiny footsteps behind me. After a few seconds of silence, I heard a sound like a door swinging. Out of the corner of my eye I saw the flower girl, John's niece, Madaline, swinging joyfully on the altar gate. It had been left open for the ceremony. Standing facing the priest, I tried not to panic, but I could hear our families and guests snickering. Oblivious to the commotion she was causing, Madaline was intent on having a good time. It was impossible to concentrate on the beautiful words the priest was sharing while this unnerving distraction was going on. At last Madaline was rescued by her aunt and the remainder of our wedding ceremony proceeded as planned.

There was only one other flaw in our memorable day. The punch we had ordered didn't arrive prior to the reception. I wasn't too concerned about it, but since my mom had taken care of the reception arrangements, she was very upset. As it turned out, it ruined her entire day. In every wedding picture, she didn't smile and looked very unhappy. Even so, I refused to allow these two events to taint the memories of our joyful wedding day. I wanted to keep this special day in my memory file for the rest of my life—and, indeed, somehow that one untarnished memory held as a kind of charmed talisman through all the difficult years to follow. Somehow I had managed to do something very right.

Love and marriage was the first major step in my exploration of independence. It was a tremendous adjustment for John and me. With different backgrounds, we joined together for a "lifetime of happiness." I had never been on my own or away from my parents for any length of time. Whatever sex education I had received consisted of information I picked up during my summer jobs picking beans. The somewhat sketchy testimonies about sex by my co-workers hadn't made the matter at all clear to me. The word "sex" had never even been whispered in my home. Looking back, there is no doubt that I was inadequately prepared for the new experience of sexual intimacy. In fact, I was scared to death of it.

My romantic schoolgirl dreams of marriage had no substance when faced with the real thing. I was so naive and unskilled in managing daily living problems that after we married I became defeated easily. Whenever I attempted new challenges that were unsuccessful, the setbacks devastated me. Each time my dreams were shattered, I internalized those failures by repeating the messages my parents gave me so loud and clear as a child, "Joann, you're worthless." As my self-image eroded further, the fear of future setbacks kept me from attempting new challenges. It was difficult not to believe those childhood messages, when all evidence seemed to confirm their validity. Little irritations each day became major problems. For instance, a minor but pronounced incident in my marriage had to do with toothpaste. My husband, John, was under the false assumption that the only way to squeeze toothpaste was from the bottom. Of course I knew that toothpaste is meant to be squeezed from the top.

This may seem like an insignificant issue to most, a lover's spat from "The Newlywed Game." But when two people lack basic communication skills, it can become magnified completely out of proportion. As it was, John didn't confront me at first. Instead, he suppressed his irritation that I didn't know the "correct" way to squeeze toothpaste. When he finally informed me, "It's not the right way, to squeeze toothpaste from the top," it was at a time when he was upset about something else. Being the insecure person that I was, my automatic response was to become defensive, "I like squeezing the tube from the top." The altercation soon escalated into a full-scale battle. This experience taught me a valuable lesson. Whenever I was angry at John, I could get even with him by squeezing the toothpaste from the top. It pushed his buttons every time.

Adjusting to the various aspects of marriage was complex for both of us. Not only did I leave my parents' home, but I left my mother's good cooking, as well as her housecleaning and laundry services. Now these chores were my new responsibilities. Simply put, I had to learn how to operate the washing machine, attempt to iron without scorching, and make an effort to keep my household expenses within my limited budget. The reality that these new obligations were mine and not my mother's any longer took a while to register with me. I soon learned that "playing house" was over. Now it was hard work. Being a wife was a major obligation that I alone was accountable for. During the 1950s, that meant I was responsible for all things that went with the title, such as cooking, which in my case left a lot to be desired. My first cake was a complete disaster.

To help supplement our budget, we lived in and managed an apartment complex for one of John's brothers. Apparently the former manager had never used the apartment oven since it was new. Without knowing this valuable information, I happily mixed the batter, following the recipe in my new cookbook. After setting the oven at the correct temperature, I tenderly put the cake in the oven. "Now that was simple," I thought; "What could go wrong?" When the timer went off, I proudly took the cake out of the oven and gazed unbelievingly at my creation. It was golden brown on top like it was supposed to be, but there was a slight problem. The cake was only one-half-inch thick. I couldn't understand it. Since appearances can be deceiving, and after I went to all of that work, I thought it was only fair that we eat it anyway.

After frosting and decorating this unusual culinary achievement, I placed it expectantly before John. You can imagine his stunned reaction. When I told him what had happened, he looked in the oven and found the broiler pan on the bottom rack. Since I had never seen a broiler pan before, I assumed it was part of the oven. My sweetie felt sorry for me, so he attempted to eat a piece. Except for a brief look of despair, he didn't die on the spot. Being a good sport, I decided it was safe to join him. After a couple of bites I swallowed my pride. I threw the cake in the trash and said that tomorrow is another day. However, neither of us were honest with each other about our feelings. Rather than hurt my pride and tell me my cake was not edible, John ignored his emotions.

Every day there were similar incidents that hindered the growth of our relationship. My insecurity and fear about making mistakes was a big problem, but most of the time I ignored them as insignificant irritations. As a result, I built up a mountain of unresolved feelings. One of John's unnerving habits was smelling his socks after he took them off in the evening. I couldn't believe it when I saw him do this the first few times. I thought, "Why would he ever doubt that his socks would smell after being on his feet in a pair of shoes all day?" Why he would want to put his nose through such an unpleasant experience I could never understand. But at that time I never told him how I felt about this unusual habit of his. Letting him continue this behavior was only one of the compromises in my marriage that I made. However, at that time in my life I wasn't aware that my undealt with feelings would surface elsewhere when I least expected it. Today when I see him smelling his socks I can tell him how I feel if it bothers me, then move on to more serious issues.

Becoming pregnant two weeks after we were married was another, rather serious development that I wasn't prepared for. Even though we hadn't made any definite plans about when to have children, we knew we wanted them someday. But we hadn't figured on "someday" being so soon after our wedding. Even though we were very apprehensive about the parental responsibility that was bestowed upon us, we were pleased about becoming parents. Neither of us knew a great deal about children, but we thought that since I had babysat a number of times without any difficulties, it couldn't be too much of a problem. Although the children that I had taken care of were no younger than age four, I didn't think that taking care of a baby would be that much different. As any parent can tell you, I was wrong again!

My desire for love and approval were the two needs which I had the most difficulty fulfilling. Since my family hadn't fostered positive feelings of love, caring, and joy during my childhood, it stood to reason that I wouldn't know how to express those feelings in my adult life as a wife and parent. John always appeared self-confident, so I couldn't let him know how frightened I was about being a mother, or how inadequate I felt as his wife. If he knew, I feared I might lose him.

Compounding the many troubles we had adjusting to marriage were early problems surrounding my pregnancy. With all three of our children I was very ill the first three to four months. I wasn't able to keep anything in my stomach for days at a time. Being pregnant was a kind of torment for me. Usually, the first three days of the week were the worst. On several occasions the doctor came to our apartment and fed me intravenously because I became so frail. Doubts about marriage and being a mother flooded my mind as I lay in bed, weakened from lack of food. I couldn't believe that this was happening to me. Since I had always had good health, constant sickness was more than an unwelcome experience for me; it was horrifying. At times death looked better.

To make matters worse, while John was away at work building homes during the day, I remained cooped up in our small, one-bedroom apartment. After having an upset stomach all day, just about five o'clock I started to feel like I might make it and could join the living again. Then John, home from work, would come into the apartment to greet me lovingly, "Honey, I'm home." As I looked at him, I would suddenly feel sick again and run for the bathroom. Poor John. That wasn't exactly the kind of greeting he was looking for.

Since we had very little time to focus on our relationship, it was a distressing period for us both. Learning to live and accept each other was difficult in itself, let alone being hampered with my pregnancy and sickness so early in our marriage. We never had the chance to concentrate on being just a couple and learning about each other. Everything happened too fast. What's more, as my body grew in size, so did my fear, my doubts, and my inadequacies. I asked myself, "What should I do with this child? How can I take care of a baby?" These and many more questions troubled me those last few months before our child came into our life.

After an extremely long and painful delivery, our first beautiful daughter arrived when I was only nineteen years old. The tiny creature, who we named Renae, terrified me completely. When I looked wonderingly at this lovely child, I realized that I knew nothing about being a parent. I was having enough problems adjusting to being a wife, so I wondered, "How can I possibly function as a good mother when I know so little?" If it hadn't been for my sister-in-law Patty and her patient guidance, I don't think that I would have survived. The first two months, Renae's crying kept us up all night. Through it all, Patty offered her help unselfishly.

There were many surprises waiting for us as we explored our new role as parents. No one ever told us the awful truth about changing diapers before we were married. Nor did we have an inkling about what was waiting for us when we first opened the diaper pail filled with soiled diapers that had been sitting there fermenting for a day or so. In order to avoid fainting from the overpowering stench of ammonia, we learned to wash the diapers much more frequently.

I'll never forget the sight of John rinsing his first soiled diaper in the toilet bowl. While holding it with two fingers and sloshing it around a bit, he put his shoe next to the toilet rim. With considerable expertise, he pulled the diaper under his sole, wringing it out as it passed between his shoe and the rim. All the while, he only touched it with his two fingers. Being 6' 1-1/2", he was able to keep a long distance between his nose and the diaper. With complete smugness, he thought this was quite an ingenious way to handle the unpleasant situation. Disposable diapers had not been invented yet, but if I had known what was in store for me and how busy I would become in the laundry room, I might have invented them and made a mint.

While I was attempting to cope with my new responsibilities as a mother, I became pregnant with our second child. Lorene was born eighteen months after our first daughter, and then eighteen months later our son Donald was born. As Catholics, John and I had been taught not to practice birth control, but we did use the rhythm method after Renae was born. Obviously this plan didn't work too well for us. After becoming pregnant three times in succession, I figured out that I was rather fertile. On the other hand, I was beginning to think that if John just looked at me I would become pregnant. Since we had all our three children early in our marriage, the future presented an entirely new set of unexpected complications to test our life together.

In four years, my life had changed dramatically, from that of a carefree teenager to that of an inexperienced mother with the responsibilities of three children, a home, and a husband. It was completely overwhelming at times. In my estimation, being a mother had very little glamour in it and was certainly not up to its advance billing. All the while, I was under so much strain that I just was not able to cope with my emotions or my daily problems. The fear of becoming pregnant again affected my desire to let John close to me. We could no longer be spontaneous or loving with each other for fear that it would lead to another pregnancy. And the time of the month that was supposed to be "safe" became shorter as my fear grew. Our once-close relationship suffered a great deal and we drifted away from each other. Since I was unable to be the loving, caring wife I wanted and expected myself to be, my guilt continued to increase.

My unrealistic expectations about being a "perfect wife" were replaced by feelings of total inadequacy. Not only did I lack skills as a wife and parent, but I lacked social skills as well. Now and then we were able to go to a movie, to the home of a friend, or to a business function. It was during this time that my social drinking started—and from that time on, I learned about the rewards of alcohol. I felt extremely inferior in the company of others, so going to parties and gatherings filled me with panic. However, after I had only one drink at a party, suddenly, with new confidence, I could talk intelligently. I became socially adept, something I had never experienced before. To me, alcohol was a harmless requirement of society that worked well for me, helping me to handle my personal inadequacies. If I had a glass of wine or two, the internal pressure would ease and take the edge off my fear. I saw nothing wrong with that at all—on the contrary, I welcomed it.

The only comfort and courage I could find in my life came in the form of alcohol. Alcohol became my faithful friend, continually reassuring me. It became my pain killer whenever I felt miserable. Each time my new-found companion soothed my agony, I could forget how rotten I felt about myself, at least for awhile. It became my escape, my refuge from facing myself and the reality of my painful existence as a worthless human being. Whenever I was hurting emotionally, I relied on my friend alcohol to take away the pain. And it worked, at least in the beginning. But as my dependency grew, I needed to use more and more alcohol to deaden the pain. It was during this time of my life that the agonizing nightmare began to take over not only me, but my family as well. No one suspected that we were slowly becoming entangled in the web of a destructive family disease which would eventually consume each one of us.

All this time, John's self-confidence had been growing steadily. His building business was prospering and he was involved in various community functions, but I felt lost, unable to separate myself from my increasing responsibilities. It seemed like we had more and more disagreements with no resolutions. Whatever the problem, we didn't understand that our conflicts with each other severely affected our three children. When they witnessed our inability to talk about our differences without becoming hostile and resentful, their vision of a happy homelife crumbled.

For a time we were our children's only basis for certainty in life. They measured and compared everything in their lives with our values. Aside from that, they looked to us for direction, love, affection, and approval, just as I had to my own parents. For a long time, their trust and faith in us went unchallenged. From the beginning of their lives, the children needed our strength to calm their insecurities. They wanted continual reassurance that everything was fine in their lives. However, in our family there was nothing that resembled stability. There was little substance on which the children could base a strong foundation of living skills. We were unable to supply their needs with the emotional security they were entitled to.

Unfortunately, John and I didn't have any ground rules set up early in our marriage. For example, when he came home after a difficult day at work, I immediately told him what his children did to me all day. He was tired and generally in no mood to hear about my problems with the children when he walked in the door, so he became sharp with me, or walked away. To further complicate the situation, I misinterpreted his actions as meaning he wasn't interested at all. If we had established a rule early on, such as John telling me, "I need thirty minutes to unwind after work; then we can talk," we would have saved ourselves misunderstandings and hurt feelings. There were so many areas in which specific rules might have eased the many differences we had in our lives.

While I experimented with alcohol as a young mother, I found it not only erased all of my emotional pain, but my physical pain as well. It comforted me when I was lonely and offered solace to me when my heart and ego were damaged. It enabled me to run away from my guilt and not look back at the loathsome creature I felt I had become.

Alcohol covered my anger that was growing daily and diminished the sorrow that saddened my spirit. I found it worked well for me once, twice, and then again and again. Each time I was drawn to this pain reliever, it trapped me in its power, so I found excuses to use it frequently. Alcohol eased my increasing despair and offered me temporary oblivion. The more I depended on it, the more I turned away from myself, my family, and the real world. What I hadn't anticipated was the amount of emotional suffering that alcohol inflicted on me, as well as my family, for so many wasted years. The loneliness, disappointments, anguish, and fear our children experienced through living in a chemical family for such a long time has left deep and painful emotional scars, and has affected their lives profoundly.

7

CHEMICAL ADDICTION/
PERSONAL ADDICTION

Whenever my husband confronted me about drinking too much I rationalized my guilt away. My frequent comeback was, "I only drink on occasion." Sometimes I replied to John, "Well, what about you? Whenever you drink, you get sick and I don't." In an instant my defenses were up and I resorted to my justifying and blaming tactics. After all, my best defense was counter-attack, a method I used often to get the pressure off of me. John didn't have a chance against my well-developed self-protection system. In a matter of seconds, I shifted the focus onto him, or whatever else was convenient to blame.

Thinking back to my personal nightmare on the road to addiction, it seems impossible that I couldn't see what was before me. I knew nothing about alcoholism nor did I know any alcoholics personally, at least any that I recognized. Therefore, I could ignore any clues regarding the destruction the disease had in store for me.

Perhaps if I had foreseen the agonizing future of becoming a victim of alcoholism, I might have changed the course of my life earlier. But even if I had been capable of seeing my future, would I really have believed that a life of addiction was my fate? Would I have believed the chaos and pain of destroyed relationships that was my destiny? Would I have accepted the vision of me hiding booze around the house, or fighting with my family? Would I have seen myself attempting to take my life to avoid dealing with myself and my emotional pain? The answer to those questions would be "no," since the blindness the disease inflicts most certainly would have kept me in the dark.

Cocktail parties and social functions caused a great deal of stress for me, so I literally had to force myself to attend these affairs. Several days before each social event, my anxiety level rose steadily, so by the time the occasion arrived, my fear was often overwhelming. However, having a drink before we departed decreased my fear noticeably. It continually amazed me how calm one drink made me feel. I believed that this was truly a miracle cure. "This must be why people drink—to feel good," I said to myself, "because it certainly doesn't taste good. And since it's so effective," I rationalized, "I'll try my new tension-reducer before we go out again." It wasn't long before I discovered this method of medicating my emotions relieved other painful feelings, as well. I had accumulated a lifetime of undealt-with feelings and my emotional pain was becoming unbearable. It seemed perfectly natural for me to use alcohol to silence the suppressed pain.

The unwritten rules I had learned in my childhood family resurfaced throughout my life in many ways. They continually affected how I related to my husband and our children, and of course, when our children reached adolescence, I imposed the same rules on them as had been imposed on me. Naturally, they rebelled against the identical unrealistic rules, just as I had done.

At times life was more than I could manage, especially when our children reached the adolescent stage one after another. They were affected by the social climate of the Sixties, demonstrating their independence by questioning everything. There was a new crisis each day, particularly when I practiced the controlling methods I was raised with. As an adolescent, as well as a parent, I used manipulation as a means to fulfill my needs. As a mother, I attempted the game of control and often became more childish than the children. Threatening and manipulating the children to do what I wanted sometimes helped to keep them in line, but as a rule, it only raised more rebellion. They sought to find their own individuality rather than live out my fantasy concerning how children needed to behave. In response, the more I tried to control them, the more they defied me.

Our unsettled lifestyle inevitably affected the children's choices in life. Even though they witnessed my alcohol abuse destroying our lives, they, too, experimented with chemicals in their teen years. Ironically, our children used it for the same reasons I did: to numb the emotional pain for awhile so they didn't have to feel miserable and worthless. Although they observed my addiction and inappropriate behavior, it didn't stop them from trying various chemicals. Thankfully those were short-lived experiments. Even though they didn't want to be like me, if our children had continued to abuse chemicals, they would probably have become like the person they despised.

Our power clash continued throughout their entire adolescence, with each of us determined to have things our own way, no matter the cost. Since I didn't know how to communicate on any level with our children, it was impossible for them to learn positive communication skills from me. In any case, we soon learned that raising adolescents was a time full of apprehension, discord and heartache, with very little joy involved for our entire family.

As my preoccupation with alcohol increased, John and I grew further and further apart. We were unable to discuss anything for five minutes without becoming defensive. Our daily lives were in continual conflict. No matter what the problem was, we argued. Whether it had to do with our children, our home, my husband's business, or ourselves, it didn't seem to matter. There were times when our anger was so intense that we seemed to hate each other.

John's work became more excessive. It was his only escape from the living hell we were going through. In reaction, our children acted out their mounting unhappiness in various ways. They refused to do their homework or neglected their chores around the house. And because they didn't know how to deal with the painful emotions they were experiencing, fighting with each other became an outlet.

The needs of our family were really no different than those of any other family. What we had always wanted was love, security, and stability. Since John and I were unable to verbally express love to our children, they became insecure and withdrew from us. The end result was that they, too, learned to suppress feelings, creating doubts concerning their emotions. Their trust in both John and me deteriorated and, in turn, increased their bewilderment concerning our expectations of them. I was unable to show love without the "assistance" of my chemical, alcohol. Somehow it was easier to tell them I loved them after a few drinks. Unfortunately, my display of "love" verified to our children that it was a meaningless expression. They knew that it was the influence of alcohol talking, not their mom.

We also wanted acceptance from one another, as well as to be respected and to be heard. However, our dreams weren't to come true, at least while the disease had control of us. Chemical addiction was dominating not only me, but it was slowly and methodically destroying our family. It was impossible to obtain any of the harmony that we saw in our healthier friends' families while we were controlled by the illness.

All through our children's teen years, John and I were, as usual, miserable and not getting along at all. We were preoccupied with ourselves and our personal problems, so we weren't able to deal effectively with the conflicts of our adolescent children. Instead, we struggled through this time of confusion and distress on our own, although at one time we did make a feeble attempt to get some professional counseling after our daughter Lorene ran away from home. She had been rebelling and couldn't stand living at home, so she ran away, hitchhiking across the state with her girlfriend, Lesa. After a time-consuming and worry-filled search for several days, John and Lesa's father found them unharmed in the next state, at the girl's mother's home. Since the police had been involved, we were required to seek help with the juvenile services in our city. The assigned counselor gave us some help regarding the various problems with the children, but we never addressed one primary issue, my alcohol addiction.

Longer periods of depression added to my misery. Even though increasing daily problems offered me ample excuses to drink, I didn't indulge during the day time through my early years of drinking. It was my opinion that I couldn't have a problem with alcohol if I abstained during the day. In any case, after the socially accepted five o'clock cocktail hour, I believed it was okay. I didn't break my self-imposed rule for many years. However, during the last few years of drinking, my mounting problems created so much internal tension that I had difficulty managing them, so of course, I moved my cocktail hour up a few hours. In recovery, I learned that since I did most of my drinking in the evenings, my body was going through withdrawal during the day. Therefore, the lack of my drug, alcohol, created more dissension and hopelessness for me.

The daytime withdrawal symptoms from alcohol further complicated all of my other problems. I became more irritable and critical with our children as well as my husband, finding fault with everything they did. I tended to over-discipline the children, while my husband under-disciplined them. Neither of us knew how to be consistent. My complete incompetence as a mother and wife continued to bewilder me. At times, I tried very hard to be patient and understanding with my family. Then, at other times, I wasn't able to cope with them at all. As my frustrations grew, it seemed that no matter how much effort I put forth, I destroyed any progress with my irrational behavior.

It was discouraging for my family in their attempts to deal with me in a reasonable manner. Through this painful time we were all becoming people we no longer recognized, preoccupied with personal despair. There were more quarrels, more verbal attacks, until we merely tolerated our mutual existence. Each one of us developed our individual symptoms of this powerful disease, yet we couldn't see that alcoholism was the real cancer behind the bitterness, which grew and killed us a little more each day.

I continually minimized and made excuses whenever my family confronted me about my negative behavior. On one occasion, our children had already eaten dinner and were downstairs studying. As I waited for John's arrival, I soothed my growing anger at his continual lateness by having several glasses of wine. After he arrived home, two hours late, I started to warm his ruined dinner, banging pans and dishes loudly in the kitchen. My anger at him had been building inside of me, and we began arguing about his frequent tardiness. John tried to explain, but I refused to accept his various excuses. Yelling in frustration, I hurled a ketchup bottle across the room at him. Protecting himself, he ducked down, as the bottle sailed passed him and through the window. After looking at the broken window, John angrily jumped off the couch and headed for me. Afraid, I ran out of the kitchen, down the hall, into our bedroom, and shut the sliding door quickly. Listening at the door, I determined that he hadn't followed me.

Later, when we had both calmed down, I slipped silently back into the kitchen. Pretending that nothing had happened, I began to clear the dishes away. However, when John confronted me, I said, as I had so many other times, "Why are you so worked up? It's no big deal." For some reason, I believed this sentence took care of any harm I had caused. After I justified my actions, John started to doubt his own perception, saying to himself, "Maybe it's really not that bad."

The unfortunate delusion that I, like all alcoholics, lived under was the rationale, "I am in control; I can stop any time I want to. I just don't want to." I called myself a "social drinker." By constantly comparing myself to others who drank far more excessively than I did, I could continue abusing my chemical. I justified, "After all, what could be wrong with something that makes me feel good? How can a few relaxing drinks be harmful? I only drink to be sociable, to have fun, to belong. Who doesn't overdo once in awhile?" These were a few automatic excuses I relied on each day to convince myself I wasn't addicted.

My stereotyped vision of an alcoholic was a hopeless derelict, a person who drank all day, every day. "And, since I don't drink during the day, I can't be alcoholic," I rationalized. In the meantime, as our socializing increased, so did the drinking rituals. John and I often had a glass of wine or a cocktail before dinner and a glass or two of wine during dinner. Then, maybe once in awhile, if we were at a party, we had a few after-dinner drinks. No matter what the occasion, I justified our increased alcohol consumption with, "Everyone does it, so there can't be any harm in it."

For years, our lives revolved around business and social occasions, so there were countless opportunities to abuse my buddy alcohol. At all the functions, alcohol was easily obtained and was socially acceptable. Not only that, we belonged to a dance club that had approximately four dances a year. Gathering for drinks and friendly conversation before the occasion, as well as after the dance, was a customary practice. Then there were the autumn football games, when we invited guests for lunch and drinks before the game. Of course, after the game we went to a local gathering spot to discuss the game, play by play, with the inevitable rounds of drinks available to console or reward us.

During these events it was easy for me to get lost in the crowd, conveniently ignoring how many drinks I was consuming. I was unable to see the hold alcohol was developing over me. Having friends over for dinner or to play cards were also acceptable drinking opportunities. Invariably, after each party or social occasion my husband and I had heated arguments. These, in turn, justified my next episode with my rarely failing friend, alcohol. I completely ignored the fact that I needed increasing amounts of alcohol to numb my constant emotional pain.

At the same time, our children were as perplexed about our disruptive behaviors as we were blind to their fears. They had no one to turn to, no one to ease their suffering as their resentments grew. Denial and suppression of feelings became their only resource for coping. Each one of our children became increasingly isolated, burying their individual misery. In order to avoid my meddling in their lives, they found other avenues of escape, such as involvement in various school projects and sports. They learned not to bring friends home for fear I would embarrass them. On the other hand, being with their friends away from home helped them avoid some of the loneliness. By denying that any problems existed, to themselves as well as to their friends, they could temporarily elude the ongoing nightmare.

Since Renae's needs weren't met at home, she found love and support from her boyfriend, Jon, and eventually became pregnant when she was sixteen. It was an extremely painful time for our entire family and we didn't deal with the situation well. Feeling guilty, I believed I had completely failed as a mother or this wouldn't have happened. Since Renae and Jon were in high school, and too young to raise a child, they did what they thought best for the baby. After listening to the input from both sets of parents, they made the heartbreaking decision to give up their baby girl for adoption. We thought that in time the pain and remorse we all felt would diminish, but in truth, it never left us. To run away from myself, as well as my terrible guilt, I found another excuse to drink my sadness away.

Sometimes I couldn't bear to think about what was in store for me at the start of each day. There was so much contention, so much unhappiness to deal with, that it was clearly overwhelming at times. Many mornings I didn't want to leave the refuge of my warm bed to face whatever crisis lay before me, but in the evenings I found alcohol allowed me to avoid looking at my inadequacy as a parent and wife.

Besides marital difficulties, John and I noticed mounting obstacles in the way of coping with our teen-agers. Shortly after each of our children received their driver's licenses, they were involved in individual car accidents. Even though they weren't hurt, I worried every time one of them used the car. At another time, Don and his friends were stopped for a traffic violation and arrested because marijuana had been found in the car. Over-reacting as usual, I knew that these terrible problems our children were having happened only because of my inadequacy as a mother.

By this time, my husband was working extremely long hours. Whenever I was left home alone, I used the "abandoned wife" role with family or anybody who listened. Even though I frequently grumbled about my loneliness and feelings of worthlessness when I was drinking, John didn't seem to hear me. He had learned to tune me out, especially when I was under the influence of alcohol.

Even after my disease was almost completely out of control, I wasn't able to identify what was dominating me. As long as I focused my anger for all of my problems at John, I didn't have to look at myself or what I had become. Aside from that, I still didn't think my drinking was a problem, so I didn't examine other options. Although John occasionally hinted that I needed professional counseling, particularly after a crisis, I completely discounted his insinuations.

One evening after consuming several drinks, John and I argued intensely about the children and the various problems they were having. Upset, I withdrew to our bedroom, calming my nerves with a few more drinks from my hidden supply. Crying and feeling extreme sadness, I decided I couldn't stand my pain any longer. Hysterically, I continued my irrational thoughts: "And when I'm gone, he'll be sorry he was so mean." After searching the bathroom cupboard, I swallowed every pill that I could find, then laid down on my bed to await the end. When John came to bed two hours later, he saw the empty bottles on the sink counter. Realizing what I had done, he angrily carried me to the car and drove to the hospital Emergency Room. After having my stomach pumped, I remained in critical condition for several hours. When I finally woke up, not only was I upset about still being alive, but I was overwhelmed with depression. The Emergency doctors emphatically suggested that I spend some time in the psychiatric ward before going home. Even though I reluctantly agreed, it didn't help me much, since I refused to become involved in the program.

For some time my family thought I was crazy, so they persuaded me to see a psychiatrist after my suicide attempt.

Several sessions were spent talking in depth about how miserable I was. After I convinced the doctor that John was the problem and not me, he took my husband aside and suggested we relax over a couple of drinks. Then the helpful doctor prescribed the currently favored fix-your-emotions drug, valium, to help my depression. One side effect of these happy pills was sleepiness, but their biggest benefit was helping me get through the daytime without shaking so much. With valium assisting me, I could make it to the five o'clock cocktail hour.

I had so many serious problems at this point that it was easy to convince the doctor that my misfortunes were not alcohol-related. One day, during my session, the psychiatrist started telling me about his conflicts with his wife and how they weren't getting along. Then he called his secretary on the phone and told her to take thirty minutes off my bill. I thought, "That's cute; what am I doing here?" Without further adieu, I left. I decided not to return, telling myself, "If he can't keep his life in order, he certainly won't help me straighten my life out." I figured neither his "help" nor the valium was needed any longer.

Our family life didn't improve after my encounter with the psychiatrist. Instead, it continued to deteriorate rapidly. We existed in pain for several more years, struggling through countless situations of crisis.

Playing mind games with each other became a destructive habit with John and me. If my husband was going to make me so miserable, I would get even with him. Undermining John and being critical of him in front of others, or taking out my frustration for my unhappy situation on both him and our children gave me some release. So I drank *at* him, and the more he tried to stop me from using alcohol, the more I used. Through it all, I didn't see that my growing bitterness was thoroughly taking control of me. The only thing that gave me any kind of peace from suffering was alcohol. It still worked for me, at least most of the time.

Since my family didn't understand me, I occasionally turned to my last few friends, talking about my misery with them. For awhile they listened. But, eventually, they tired of my constant complaining about how my family took advantage of me or their lack of appreciation for my noble efforts toward them. Without knowing it, I had now moved into the addictive characteristic known as the "martyr syndrome."

During my drinking years, I played this part frequently to gain compassion for my miserable plight. Feeling sorry for myself as the persecuted, misunderstood martyr gave me a certain amount of personal power. Concentrating on my unfortunate past, I used it as an excuse to feel miserable. Feeling pity for myself enabled me to avoid attempting any new challenges. Sometimes I said to myself, "Look at what happened to me—isn't it terrible? Please feel sorry for me." This kind of attitude was meant to win sympathy and attention from others, but it didn't work. Continually moaning to friends and family did nothing but drive them all away, leaving me a bitter, lonely, and shame-filled human being. Any time I was confronted by my family about performing the martyr role, I became defensive. In reaction, I wept and condemned, all the while using my chemical to soothe my emotions.

Since I wasn't coping with life or emotions, my level of stress increased. Consequently, I developed other illnesses that were directly due to stress, such as backaches, headaches, and fatigue. To add to those problems, I wouldn't eat properly, or exercise, so I continued to lose weight, neglecting myself not only emotionally, but physically as well. I became more irrational and tense. During those days, whatever cooking I attempted generally consisted of opening a variety of cans and heating the contents. By now I was shaking so badly during the day that it affected my performance of simple tasks, such as setting the table, ironing, and particularly writing letters.

Neither of us realized it, but by this time John had acquired a position of power. My husband's goals had always been directed toward the good of our family. As well as being our financial provider, he wanted the best for us, including peace, happiness, and love. Not only did he acquire the role of superperson for the family, but in his work as well. He was generous with his employees, helping them when the need arose. Frequently he worked to appease a frantic customer. Often he became my guardian angel, sheltering the family from embarrassment with employees, friends, and acquaintances concerning my behavior. Without being aware of it, his caretaking actions for the family became almost as compulsive as my alcoholic behavior.

Although John pretended to the world that his life was sane, it became an effort to reinforce the lies to his friends and associates that everything was fine. Occasionally his worries plagued him with sleepless nights and fatigue. He kept thinking to himself, "If only Joann didn't drink. If only the children wouldn't fight—then everything would be all right." The "if only" statements enabled him to hang on and retain the everlasting hope that things would somehow change for the better—someday.

Overwhelmed with our ongoing family distress, John finally looked in the yellow pages of the phone book for help. He decided to meet with a local minister who worked in the field of alcoholism. With dark glasses on, John drove into the parking lot of the church. Before getting out of the car, he carefully looked around to see if there was anyone he knew walking about. Then he quickly went into the building for a meeting with the minister. After a few minutes, he left with a handful of brochures containing alcoholism information. With his dark glasses on, he inspected the parking lot for familiar faces, but, seeing no one, he got into the car, drove home, and went into the house. He placed a few pamphlets in strategic places, then put the rest of the literature in the filing cabinet in his office.

When I saw one of the brochures on the kitchen counter and glanced at the listed symptoms of alcoholism, my denial system was activated. I would show him that I didn't have a problem and I certainly wouldn't display any of the described symptoms. "After all," I told myself, "I'm not the sick one in the family; it's John and the kids who are the problem."

8

CHEMICAL FAMILY

Dᴜʀɪɴɢ ᴛʜᴇ ʟᴀᴛᴇ sᴛᴀɢᴇs of my disease, I was admitted to the hospital for a vaginal hysterectomy. It was supposed to be a simple procedure, but as it turned out, I had other severe problems, requiring the doctor to operate. Several days later, there were internal complications which resulted in a blocked and twisted intestine. After becoming violently ill, I had to be rushed to Emergency for additional surgery. When I became conscious in Intensive Care, besides having one scar from the first surgery, I now had another six-inch scar on my stomach and rib cage. Seeing the results, I began to cry, not just because of the pain but because I felt truly ugly now. With no appetite, I became extremely weak, so it was necessary to be fed through my veins for three to four weeks. One day when John was visiting, my doctor suggested, "John, bring in some small bottles of wine to help increase Joann's appetite." That's what every alcoholic needs, a thoughtful doctor. Even though my husband was suspicious and surmised that this was my idea, he brought the wine anyway. Of course, it didn't help my desire to eat, since I guzzled down the wine when no one was looking.

In a severely depressed state, I left the hospital over a month later. I felt physically repulsive and more disheartened about life than ever. Because of my hideous scars, I believed John didn't want to have anything to do with me. Using that as another excuse, I relied more and more on alcohol to subdue my pain.

As I recuperated, my level of drinking increased. The complete communication breakdown in our family added to the confusion about our desperate situation. Besides suppressing our emotional desires, we had an ongoing fear of discussing the "family problem" in our home, as well as outside of the home, because I might go into a drinking rage. The expression of all understanding and compassion for each other was completely disappearing.

Although I came from a dysfunctional home, I was unaware that the lifestyle of negativity and denial that I had become accustomed to wasn't a normal living situation. It was the only way I knew how to live, so by the time my disease had fully developed, my denial system was even more firmly entrenched. Denial was the fine line that kept me from falling apart completely and facing the truth. It was the only way to protect myself from detection and acknowledgment that I needed help. As long as I could dismiss my negative behavior, I could convince others, myself included, that I really didn't have a problem with alcohol.

Denial was an obstacle for our entire family. As we hid from our plight for years, it kept us from seeing that we were held prisoner by the disease. More observant friends, along with our parents, were aware that unhealthy transformations were occurring in our family. Baffled, they saw our personalities alter, tempers flare, and patience deteriorate. My friend Sara kept asking me, "What is happening to your family?" I mumbled some feeble explanation, but never admitted to her, or myself, that the real problem was alcohol. Even with constant turmoil surrounding us, we were unable to overcome our fear and clarify the ordeal our family was experiencing. Instead, we withdrew further from our pain, from each other, from friends and family, as a means of survival.

To present some semblance of normalcy to the outside world, I kept trying to reassure everyone that I was fine. Even during the last unbalanced years, I had moments of sanity. There was the time when my son Don, in his early teens, decided to risk embarrassment and invite some of his school friends to stay overnight one weekend. Eager to prove myself worthy, I attempted to calm his apprehensions. Then, silently, I vowed to myself, "I will be a responsible mother and not drink."

As I prepared some snacks and goodies for the boys during the day, I felt my stress rising, yet I reassured myself that I could handle one drink. With my confidence restored, I thought, "It's almost fun being productive again." When everyone arrived at seven in the evening, Don was nervous, afraid that I would embarrass him in front of his friends. By this time my nerves were screaming, "Soothe me, give me more medication." Giving in, it wasn't long before my vow to have only one drink had been broken a number of times.

John knew I had been drinking, so after I took the food down to the boys in the activity room, he suggested I remain upstairs. Since I believed I was in complete control, I became furious with him for implying that I was drunk. As we argued, our voices became louder and louder. Don could hear us downstairs, so he turned up the music and shut the hall door. Angrily, I grabbed my purse and keys, left the house, and decided to go to a movie. To everyone's relief, I didn't return until John and the boys were sleeping. The next morning I felt bad about ruining Don's party and so ashamed that I couldn't face him. No one brought up my behavior, so I decided not to, either. However, I berated myself for not being able to fulfill a simple need of my son—to have a sober mother who he could love and respect.

While the disease advanced, John and our children acquired various destructive tendencies, much like mine, which I learned in treatment are referred to as co-dependency traits. As I developed mood swings and became defensive, so did my family. As I blamed my family for my problems, they also held me responsible for their personal behavior, their depression, and their apparent loss of control. They covered up, denied, and lied, just as I had done. While I focused on alcohol to relieve my pain, my family's addiction to controlling me and my drinking increased.

The emotional isolation that each one in our family suffered resulted in suppression of both positive and negative feelings for one another. Not knowing how to cope, our daily life became a pattern of unending confrontation. It was sad that whatever sensitivity we once had for each other's needs was no longer apparent. The love we had once experienced was now hidden from view, with anger and resentment taking its place.

Though the disease pulled us away from each other, an invisible bond still tied us to one another. Leaving the situation helped some, but we were inevitably drawn back into the devastation. Through it all, John felt resentment about the overwhelming burden of managing all the daily conflicts our family was experiencing. Not only did he want to escape from our life of pain, but so did the children.

It became a full time job to maintain myself in public so that our family secret could remain hidden. To keep from drawing undue attention to myself, I traveled to different liquor stores and grocery stores to buy vodka and wine. I avoided running short of my supply on the weekend by placing small containers of alcohol in various strategic hiding places in our home. I rationalized that I had to do this since my husband was always watching me. Then there were the many times when I forgot where I hid my bottles.

John knew I was concealing booze, so we played the hide-and-seek game. As he discovered my hiding places, I was forced to find new "secret" places. He didn't seem to understand that when life was stressful I needed some reinforcement. Therefore, I didn't want a hassle each time I required some courage.

We always kept a supply of liquor in the kitchen cupboard, which we used to entertain our friends. During the occasions when my personal supply ran low, I "borrowed" a few ounces from some of the bottles. Of course, I was careful to refill the bottles with water to the mark my husband had previously made. When we served drinks to our guests, in my delusion I figured they wouldn't be aware that they were drinking mostly water.

Cooking with wine was a gourmet practice that I frequently used whenever I was in the mood to cook. It seemed reasonable to me to pour some measured wine into my culinary delight and then reward myself with a sip, or two, or three, for my ingenious creation.

As John became more preoccupied with trying to control my alcohol consumption, he constantly checked my hiding places for booze. And, as a result, I was forced to find new secret spots. To make matters worse, he hovered over me at social functions, watching my alcohol consumption. Through the years, he wasn't able to see his own delusion in thinking that he could personally stop the escalation of the disease. Frustrated, John typically blamed other influences for the majority of my problems, such as the lack of a job outside of our home or some hobbies to occupy my time.

Our children developed the rescuing technique of justifying my behavior when talking with friends. "My mom's got the flu today; that's why she looks so bad." Or, "Mom's crabby because my parents argued last night," were just a couple of their excuses. It was easier for my family to delude themselves that these "reasons" were the primary problem that caused my crazy behaviors, not my drinking. In this way, they were able to avoid the truth, that my addiction to alcohol was the real poison that was intent on annihilating our family.

To keep my addiction going, I had to plan my days carefully. Much of my time was spent going to various stores to buy alcohol. After arriving back at home, I filled my little bottles and stashed them in the bedroom, the bathroom, the office, or the laundryroom. My memory was now fading, so I wrote myself notes that indicated my hiding places. Then, after temporarily concealing the empty bottles at home, I needed to handle the problem of permanent disposal for my empties. Alcoholics have to be resourceful to survive, so I sacked up my bottles and dropped them in grocery store dumpsters, or Goodwill boxes around town. I certainly didn't want the evidence found in my garbage can, allowing the garbage man to learn about my "secret." During the many times that I lied to myself and others, I find it astonishing that I didn't suspect my actions weren't normal behavior. It simply did not occur to me that if I didn't have a problem with alcohol, I wouldn't be rushing around covering my tracks so diligently.

Trying to cut down my alcohol consumption didn't seem to help either. Near the last years of my close-to-seven-year relationship with alcohol, I tried several times to stop on my own. Each morning, I vowed to myself, "I won't drink today," yet each time I relented, losing my will to the powerful grip of my alcoholism. I was blind to the fact that I had lost any control over whether I drank or didn't drink. I didn't see that my demanding friend, alcohol, had made me its slave. With self-hate growing, I despised my inability to stop the madness that devoured my family and me.

As life's pressures continued to mount, John's faith that he could stop my drinking dwindled away. He wondered whether he should risk expanding his building business, since there was a growing demand for quality homes in our area. However, he didn't have much enthusiasm for meeting the challenge, because it looked like our marriage was over. Besides that, concern for the welfare of the children if we separated was on his mind constantly.

Even though the disease had dominated us for so long, we had somehow survived this far. Acting and reacting to each other in dependent and co-dependant behaviors had taken its terrible toll. At this point, hope was but an illusion, a fading dream, that life would ever be different. Our vision that we could love each other once again and be a happy, close family was completely vanishing.

Completely isolating myself by now, I refused to depart from the house, except to buy alcohol and supplies. My family was relieved to leave me home so that I wouldn't humiliate them. Using every occasion as an excuse to drink, I told myself, "It's okay to have just one drink to calm my nerves," but it rarely stopped with one drink. As I soothed my rage at life and the world with alcohol, my anger was vented on John as I shouted frequently, "I hate you." When our children tried to intercede, I would turn on them, telling them, "The world is a rotten place, full of pain," as I attempted to pull them down to my level of despondency. As our love turned into hate, we all became victims in a nightmare of desolation that seemed endless.

Too often, when I was drinking, I had the expectation that my family would love me no matter what hurts I inflicted upon them. I continually asked my family for forgiveness concerning my display of negative behavior. Though I appeared sincere, they had heard me say the phrase, "I'm sorry," so many times that the words meant nothing. I gave my usual assurance, "I promise never to lose control again." Each time it happened, my family longed to believe that this time my vow was true.

Whenever my family observed my love on one day and then the love withdrawn on another, they were left with emptiness and confusion. It caused them to pull away from me, further widening the gap between us. Even throughout the years of pain and drinking, I searched for a way to re-establish our lost love by being extra accommodating. In that way, I could avoid my guilt for awhile.

Even though we were miserable and dysfunctional, my family wanted me to get better, to stop destroying myself with alcohol. The hope that I would soon change my behavior still kept them going. The art of assuring my family, "Everything is fine and you have nothing to worry about," was a technique that I knew so well. At times, John literally despised me for making his life so unbearable, but deep down inside, buried under the suffering, a persistent determination kept his hope alive. Our love had been restricted by so much emotional pain that we no longer knew if any still existed.

One evening, I was in a particularly miserable mood, so I had indulged in several drinks before John and I attended a friend's party. Throughout the night we drank far too much, trying to forget our pain. About two in the morning, we drove home in silence, then began arguing as we entered the house. The alcohol fed my wrath, allowing some of my anger to spill out on John. Refusing to listen to my tirade, he closed the door to the bathroom.

Furious at him, I ran out of the house, started the car, and raced down the driveway. With tears flowing down my face, I sped across town and up a winding road in the hills. After driving several miles with no traffic to bother me, I stopped the car and let my pain run free. Turning the car around, I decided I didn't want to live. Determined to end my pain, I headed down the hill, winding back and forth across the highway at a reckless speed. I was playing chicken with myself, coming closer and closer to the edge of the ravine at each turn. Near the bottom of the hill, I closed my eyes and let go of the wheel.

When I woke up, the car had stopped and I heard my husband shouting angrily at me. It seems that the car had somehow jumped a ditch and was suspended over it, balancing on its wheels. He was furious that I had damaged the car. Some men stopped to help, so in the confusion, I scrambled out the other side of the car and ran across the road toward a darkened school. In the meantime, the men helped John get the car back on the side of the road. After parking the car, he started searching for me. In the distance, I could hear him calling my name as I sat cowering in a darkened doorway. After some time, there was a long period of silence. By now I was sobering up and cold, so when I felt it was safe, I started the long walk home. Fortunately, I made it home before the dawn and the neighbors awakened. John was asleep by now, so I lay on the couch to wait for the children to get up. I figured he wouldn't make a scene in front of them.

The children were watching cartoons and I was getting breakfast when John walked into the kitchen. Glaring at me, he sat down, eating in silence. Neither of us had the energy to start arguing again, so we pretended the night never happened. Even though I felt guilty about my behavior, it didn't erase my death wish, but increased my depression.

John tried various tactics to bring me out of my depression, but I refused to cooperate with him. Instead, I used more alcohol, not realizing that it was a depressant. Although John didn't know how to handle my depressive moods, he still didn't leave me. He felt hopeless at times, yet he hadn't given up completely. While my disease grew, so did John's addiction to trying to change my behavior and to controlling my drinking. It became a fixation with him, just as my alcohol had become a preoccupation with me. He had vowed to protect forever this so-called "relationship" we had had since the day we were married, yet at other times he wondered why he remained, other than because of the children. In order to help him avoid our hopeless situation, John began to spend more time away from the house, doing things with our children and friends, trying to make up for our dismal life. Through it all, he knew he had to keep things together; there was no one else.

When John was home, he tried to get me to eat something nourishing, since I was nothing but skin and bones by now. Eating food dulled the numbing effects of alcohol, so I either ate very little, or filled up on unhealthy snacks. I firmly believed that my family would be better off without me. In desperation, after I had been drinking heavily, I drove to a nearby cemetery. Sitting beside a tombstone, I made another serious attempt to end my painful journey by slashing my left wrist deeply with a hair-cutting razor. This time I was determined to die. Even though I lost a lot of blood, I didn't succeed, because someone found me and rushed me to the hospital. When the anesthetic wore off, I found myself unable to move, strapped to a hospital bed in a straight-jacket. Again I had bungled my attempt to find freedom from myself. To add to my problems, my recovery period from the repair surgery was lengthy, leaving permanent damage to my arm.

Why my family took me back when I had put them through hell, I will never quite understand. I was so ashamed when I went home. Every morning after awakening, I immediately became immersed in more guilt. Then the nightmare would begin all over again. There seemed to be no escape, no relief from my agonizing existence, other than death. Thoughts about different methods to end my life were on my mind constantly. Several times in the next couple of years I overdosed on pills to escape my torment and free my family. I wanted to die, to end my nightmare. I could go on no longer. Each time I awoke in the hospital, I became more despondent than ever. Whenever I attempted to finish my agonizing existence, something prevented me from fulfilling my desire.

John realized that my disease was extremely critical now. His agony for our family's hopeless state persisted until it broke through his protective barriers. With the final conclusion approaching, he saw that our family was completely shattered, so he attempted to break out of our life of torment. At last the time had come when he could endure no more. He was desperate. He sought additional information about the paralyzing disease of chemical dependency and co-dependency that was killing us all. Then another crisis opened the door for him. After experiencing a bad fall in the garage, I ended up in the hospital to be checked for broken bones. While John was discussing my physical condition with the family doctor, he finally disclosed the terrible secret he had carried for so long. As the doctor listened and offered supportive suggestions, John found new hope.

9

TREATMENT—
RECOVERY BEGINS

God grant me serenity to accept
the things I cannot change,
courage to change the things I can,
and wisdom to know the difference.

SHORTLY AFTER my admission to treatment, nurse Mary Ann gave me a small book with the Serenity Prayer in it. In a soothing voice she told me, "I know you're upset, Joann, but if you repeat the prayer several times, the healing words will ease your resentments." Still reeling from the trauma of my intervention, I reluctantly took the book. After she left my room, I read the prayer, thinking it couldn't hurt. Although I would never admit it to anyone, she was right. I did feel a bit better after reciting the words. Without delay, my addictive thinking revived, "If it works once, lots of times works better." After the agitation of the last few days, I desperately needed something to quiet my smoldering anger, so I restated the prayer a number of times.

When I finally ventured from my room again, I saw at every turn the Twelve Steps of Alcoholics Anonymous plastered on the walls of the treatment center. The first step's words wouldn't leave my mind. After it played over and over in my subconscious like a broken record, I realized the honesty of those powerful words. It was true, my life had become uncontrollable and I couldn't fight the power that alcohol had over me.

There was nothing to do while the other patients were in group, and since I was bored looking at the four walls of my room, I wandered down the hall. Curious to know why the entire treatment staff was so enthralled with the "steps," I started reading the entire twelve steps.

Somewhat in awe about the powerful pledge, I hurried back to my room before anyone caught me reading them. Even in the security of my room, the words followed me and refused to leave my mind. Thinking about the steps, two things were apparent to me. First, I realized that I didn't fully understand them, and second, I was frightened at the treatment expectations of following the steps. I thought to myself, "It's all too confusing. Maybe Sam, the man with the funny hair, can tell me what it's all about."

Patients were expected to get involved with the treatment program almost immediately, so I didn't have much time to feel sorry for myself. Although treatment wasn't as terrible as I thought it would be, it did turn out to be far more influential than I expected. I had so many new things to grasp that I often felt overwhelmed by the magnitude of the changes that I needed to make. Even though the group therapy sessions were the most traumatic part of treatment for me, they were ultimately the most beneficial.

The group sessions always ended with the Serenity Prayer. The portion of the prayer that impressed me the most was the part about "changing the things I can about myself and accepting the things I cannot change." Of course, "having the wisdom to know the difference" was a key part, too. Learning to accept myself for what I am, and not what I would like to be, eventually helped me find the inner peace I was searching for. I realized it was a simple yet important philosophy for me to adopt in furthering my personal growth. To be sure, my work was cut out for me.

As I explored recovery, learning about the disease of alcoholism, my blinders suddenly disappeared. It became clear to me that our entire family had been in denial for many years about how much we had been affected by my drinking. We hadn't realized the mental distress that each of us developed in this environment of crisis was a burden which had to be dealt with. If we were ever to recover from the disease, it was necessary to understand that the destructive illness had contaminated each one in our family, disabling us all and making us completely vulnerable. Now I was virtually being forced to open my eyes and look at all of the unpleasant facts that I had been trying to escape.

It was really the threat of losing my husband and my family, along with whatever love they had left for me, that made me finally realize that I had to do something about my problem. Combining my strong instinct for survival and the benefit of family support, I saw there was a possibility of overcoming my addiction to alcohol.

There were so many new terms, slogans, and words to learn that I had difficulty sorting them out. It was like being in a different country, trying to understand a new dialect. The staff and patients talked about dysfunctional this and dysfunctional that all the time. Not only did the word seem to fit in every conversation, but it was the perfect description of my past life.

Through the years of recovery I learned a great deal about the family system, and later I wrote a book about my findings, called *Chemical Family*. (In the book I cover details in depth concerning the various roles family members develop in a Chemical Family.) It is a system in which each person is affected by the chemical dependence of one or more people. It has identical symptoms of a dysfunctional family, with the same detrimental behavior patterns displayed. However, these behaviors are magnified in chemical families, allowing the unhealthy symptoms to become even more bizarre and confusing as the disease of addiction progresses.

Everyone in our family had developed individual family roles that are created, to some extent, in all families of addiction. My husband had acquired the role of Prime Enabler, one who continually rescued me from suffering the consequences of my addictive behavior. In order for him to recover, he had to stop enabling.

Our children also obtained specific traits throughout my drinking years. One of the characteristics that our oldest daughter, Renae, the Achiever Child, had developed, was excessive goal achievement in order to please us, her parents. Lorene, our middle daughter, the Problem Child, searched continuously for attention by using unacceptable actions to keep us from becoming close to her. Then there was our youngest son, Don, the Comic Child, who used various ways to be noticed by using humor or disruptive behavior.

Besides me, each member of our family needed treatment to convert our ingrained dysfunctional family roles from negative to positive characteristics. Our children, who grew up with these personality-changing roles, have had a difficult time becoming aware of the specific changes necessary for them to make in their own recovery from the disease. They each have their own personal story of recovery to tell.

At the beginning of recovery, everything in our new life was unfamiliar, particularly the confusion concerning what new role each of us in the family needed to adopt. We knew we had to transform our dysfunctional roles into healthier ones, but we weren't sure how to accomplish this.

While our family was receiving treatment, we learned that in both the chemical family and dysfunctional family systems, the normal response for family members was to isolate themselves and suppress their feelings. In addition, we lacked knowledge about satisfying our personal needs and knew little about communicating with another. It became clear to me that my family life was a duplication of my childhood life. The only difference between the two systems was that chemicals were not a problem with my family while I was growing up.

In my dysfunctional family, my individual needs weren't met, nor did I know how to achieve fulfillment of my basic desires. One day in group, counselor Sam told me, "Joann, make a list of your needs." Puzzled, I replied, "But I don't know what my needs are. I never thought about them before." After struggling for hours, trying to come up with a list, I was finally able to define a few. I wanted love and affection, to be a valuable human being, and for people to respect me. The next day Sam commended me for my examples, "Good job. Now add fifteen more needs to your list." Throwing eye daggers at him didn't bother him in the least. After six more agonizing hours, I finished my assignment.

The next day I revealed my new additions in group. One was my need to make my own decisions, another was to praise myself instead of being negative, also to set more realistic goals and to accept my setbacks as part of my humanness. As I looked at my entire list, it surprised me that there were so many that I hadn't been aware of. One major need was finding inner peace, along with spiritual peace. Other needs I required were self-confidence, to express myself, to accept my feelings, as well as to cope with my emotions. Additional important needs that I came in touch with were to have responsibility and self-acceptance, to trust, to have fun, to reward myself, and to give myself praise. Somewhat overwhelmed, I could see that I had done very little in the past to enhance my personal requirements.

All my life I had tried to fulfill my individual needs without really knowing them. Actually, I discovered that my longings were no different than those of my fellow group members. As we talked about our lists in group, I realized that whatever my personal wants were, I had an inner desire to satisfy those basic necessities the best way I knew how. Unfortunately, I had found the harmful methods of alcohol and manipulation to gain self-fulfillment; therefore, I ended up hurting myself even further.

Comparing myself with others was another strong deterrent to getting my needs met. Each time I made a destructive, self-defeating comparison to someone I envied and placed above myself, my meager supply of self-worth deteriorated more. A friend of mine, Lucy, was an articulate speaker and I envied her talents a lot. For years, every time I heard her lecture or speak at a meeting, I berated myself for not being able to be as expressive. In treatment, I realized that as long as I hung onto those old beliefs and destructive habits, I would never be able to improve my self-image.

Reflecting on my new goals, it seemed that while I was in treatment, it might be a good time for me to seriously work on changing my self-image. One day in group, Sam assigned me the task of doing affirmations, that is, giving positive statements to myself every day in order to improve my self-image. As I repeated to myself positive affirmations like, "You are a good person," or "You did a good job," my self-acceptance increased. Becoming an optimist, telling myself that I could achieve goals beyond my reach, was real progress, and a vital step for me. It was time to stop being so hard on myself and to accept that I am a human being with imperfections. Sam told me to look in the mirror several times a day and tell myself, "I am a beautiful person."

At first I felt silly, laughing as I repeated the words. However, as I practiced saying the unfamiliar phrase each day, I became more comfortable. After a few weeks, I felt so much better about myself that it was truly remarkable. I realized that whenever I relaxed my rigidity and attempted a new challenge, I was able to loosen the bonds that tied me to my childhood's unrealistic demands. With the reawakening of my self-respect in treatment, my life definitely improved. As I nurtured myself with the love of my family, my group, and my counselor, the opportunity to become the person I had always wanted to be came within my grasp.

At the beginning of my personal investigation, during and following treatment, I needed to clarify my feelings and actions to better understand my own nature. It was necessary for me to examine various past events in my life, as well as take a look at my values and what I believed to be truth. As I uncovered the different elements, I had to continually remind myself that it was essential to examine all parts of my life, then deal with each one, no matter how much it hurt. This was very hard, since I was used to running away from unpleasantness. At times, the fear of going through more emotional suffering in the future hindered my ongoing pursuit of inner contentment. As my recovery developed, I found that personal growth was extremely complex, but not impossible. Sometimes I wondered if I would ever feel at ease with myself, or if I would find the love and acceptance I wanted so desperately.

Although I have gone through frustrating situations and painful rebuffs in my attempt to obtain affection and recognition from others, I have since learned that the lower my self-image is, the more devastating the rejection is when it comes. Another discovery I made is that, in order for me to fulfill my need for the love and respect of others, it must first start with me. I have to give *myself* the love and respect I want from others. Over and over I need to reinforce that

I am okay, that I like myself. I certainly can't expect others to bolster my personal growth when I refrain from self-nurturing expressions.

After several weeks of group therapy and lectures, I discovered that what I really wanted was to be in control of my life. I realized that in the dysfunctional system I came from, I constantly felt out of control. The majority of the time, I was inclined to focus on my incompetencies, even though I appeared self-assured on the outside in the company of others. Now I understood that my prerecorded childhood messages were concealed in my subconscious, ready to resurface throughout my life whenever I was threatened. Therefore, when life's events did not turn out the way I wanted them to, I automatically reverted back to the imbedded pessimistic failure message, "You can't do anything right."

Even though I didn't have the alcohol to cloud my vision anymore, I had problems grasping that I was an individual, different from all other human beings. No matter how hard I tried, I would never be anyone else but me. I was stuck with myself, whether I liked it or not, so rather than complain about my problems and character defects, I needed to learn to do my best with what I had been blessed with.

Finding out who I was, the genetics and history of my family, and why I behaved in specific ways, was suddenly important to me. It was going to be a huge task, unraveling the threads of the past, but I knew it was necessary for my recovery.

Although the required treatment stay for a patient was eight weeks, I stayed nine. My counselor believed that another week of therapy would be beneficial for me, so after some persuasion, I decided to follow his advice. As it turned out, the extra week was a special healing time, filled with peace and emotional growth. Since my personal pressures had been reduced, I felt more relaxed, which allowed me to gain new insights into myself. This was the closest I had ever been to complete happiness, and it was great.

At last, my final day in treatment arrived. I couldn't believe that this monumental day had come. It seemed so long ago when I had reluctantly been all but shoved through the front doors. At that time, I had thought eight weeks sounded like an eternity. Now it was time to leave and I didn't want to go. I was afraid to leave the security of the protective walls surrounding Serenity Lane to face the world. My concluding moments as a patient were upon me.

The custom at "S.L.U." at graduation time was to have patients, friends, and family gather in the lecture hall during the weekly Monday evening get-together to share their thoughts and emotions about their treatment experience. The event was usually a deeply moving experience for everyone involved. Now it was my turn. I was terrified of standing up in front of the large group, but the words of my heartfelt thanks and appreciation went out to everyone who had helped my transformation and recovery occur. It wasn't long before my emotions caught up with me and tears of joy, mixed with sadness, began to flow. I wanted to say so much more, but the words stuck in my throat and I couldn't go on.

After sitting down, I reflected further on my unspoken thoughts. My gratitude was overwhelming. There just were no words that came close to expressing my joy at being alive. Suddenly, I realized that I was one of the fortunate ones; so many never find help. In treatment I discovered that I had a better, more secure, and happier life available to me. Even though the many problems I encountered in treatment were frequently overwhelming, I had a powerful new desire to substitute my misery for happiness. After my passion to recover took hold, it instilled in my heart and soul a strong willingness to rebuild my life to make this change possible. Everyone I met while I was in treatment had given me so much, making this wonderful moment possible. To this day, each time I think about my appreciation, my emotions and tears are not far behind.

After treatment, it was time for John and me to move into the next phase of our recovery, called aftercare. In order to help deal with life after treatment, we were to participate in special therapy groups for fifteen weeks. Attending aftercare group once a week with John was an essential part of our recovery plan. Although I was completely terrified to be on my own, away from the safety of the treatment center, I felt excited to start a new way of living. Many problems waited for me at home with my family, but if I could deal with them individually, I believed I could make it.

Unrealistically, I wanted the growth of five years of sobriety immediately after leaving treatment, but I soon found that recovery comes in its own time. Fear of relapse kept me running daily to the haven of Serenity Lane, where I found comfort, honesty, and wisdom to keep me going. I was safe within those walls, protected from the dysfunctional world, consoled with so much support.

Learning how to manage life each day in the real world was much more complex than John and I imagined. To be able to talk about unexpected problems with our aftercare group each week helped us a lot. Practicing what we had absorbed in treatment was much easier when we had the support of our group. Since each person in the group was going through similar problems, it was a great benefit for us to see how other couples coped with the same recovery obstacles of developing healthy communication and relationships. Deciding whether to have alcohol in our home or serve it to guests was a primary concern. One of the group members, Karen, said, "I don't think serving alcohol at home will be a problem for me." Some of the group members agreed with her, but I was uncomfortable with the idea of such easy access to my poison, so John and I elected not to have it around. We also learned how others in the group handled going to social situations where alcohol was served. The most common strategy was to have a self-protection plan ready to implement when we were in a situation where alcohol was available.

Whenever I was afraid to talk to John about my emotions on a one-to-one basis, I found I could discuss my feelings and the difficulties we were having, in our group. It helped a great deal to have our aftercare counselor facilitate the group and give us feedback. Both the group and our counselor gave us a great deal of help. Our aftercare groups were not quite as confrontive as the inpatient sessions had been, and since John and I were working hard to change, we were more open to suggestions. During the three months of aftercare, I gained considerable insight into both my husband and myself. By the time we were ready to leave our group, we had both developed some stability in our recovery. Even so, it was hard for me to let go of the comfort and support of my "home group," but I knew that if I wanted to continue growing, it was necessary.

While our trust in each other slowly renewed itself, John and I could feel our love, which had lain dormant for so long, gradually returning. We never wanted to lose that love again. We wanted so much to reclaim our marriage and to make our relationship the joyful and meaningful companionship that we had once dreamed was possible.

Even though our work on our marriage occupied most of our time, I needed to take charge of my life in other areas. I had to examine various ways to reduce my inner stress. Besides learning to process my feelings more appropriately, I needed to focus on eating a balanced diet and exercising regularly. In order to handle my life more effectively, I had a critical need to get enough rest and to avoid becoming involved in more projects than I was capable of handling. Giving myself praise or a reward of some kind for all of the "right" things that I accomplished each day helped me to rebuild my self-image. Still, I found it hard and unfamiliar to give myself pats on the back.

Now and then, some of my neglected issues from the past surfaced. When I least expected it, some stifled, painful feelings regarding a specific event emerged. Occasionally I questioned the value of putting myself through the process of struggling with my emotions, but each time it happened, I knew the answers in my heart. In order to be free, I needed to acknowledge the pain and work through my emotions surrounding each incident.

One particularly painful occasion happened when I had been sober for more than six years, while I attended a Claudia Black seminar with some colleagues from work. The focus was on issues regarding adult children of alcoholics. By this time in my recovery, I had already dealt with many problems, so I thought there were no significant areas left for me to take care of. As the speaker discussed the common childhood suppressions and showed some slides of children's drawings, I suddenly started falling apart emotionally. Tears began to flow, and soon I was unable to stop sobbing. My close friends, Lois and Leroy, were with me and were concerned, yet sensitive to my hurt. Their nurturing compassion helped me finally gain control of myself. I was completely confused about what was happening to me, as well as embarrassed about my display in front of so many people, but I started the painful process of sorting through my emotions, trying to discover what triggered my hurt.

Somewhere deep inside of me, the restrained trauma surrounding some sexual abuse that I had endured as a small child suddenly emerged, as I recalled lying on my bed when I was about five, crying, trying to hold back my terror. I could remember hearing the whispered threat of bodily harm if I talked to anyone about the abuse. Sobbing, I recalled how I would lie in my bed, rigid with shame, with tears flowing down my face as I was being abused. I could feel the terrible shame and degradation, as if it had just occurred. Then the vision faded into nothing. It was replaced by the sight of me pretending I was asleep to protect myself from more abuse. Another time I hid in the closet, hoping not to be discovered. At a different time I could see the sun shining, and I was sitting at the kitchen table with my parents. Every time I gathered my courage together to tell them what had happened, paralyzing fear prevented my disclosure. Somehow I knew they would blame me. It was hard to believe that those appalling incidents had been completely repressed from my conscious mind for so many years.

Even though recalling the hidden wounds was frightening to me, I knew that it was time to be done with another piece of the past. The next day I went to Sam, my treatment counselor, and talked about the incidents and my feelings surrounding them until the pain finally subsided. During the next few weeks I was able to process my emotions and understand more clearly how the sexual abuse had affected me all of my life. Particularly, my marriage had suffered a great deal as a result of my suppressed shame and fear about intimacy. Eventually, through many hours of therapy, I was able to free myself from the heavy burden and move on with my life. Another enormous weight had been lifted from my heart.

There have been other minor traumas that have surfaced since that time. In each instance, I was fearful to sort through the revived emotional pain, which had been out of reach for so many years. But I had a clear choice now of whether to move forward into positive growth or move back into the despair of the disease. What I found was when I talked openly about my pain as it surfaced, my self-confidence and courage grew, allowing me to become liberated. I didn't have to be alone anymore unless I chose to.

What was once the "normal" situation of chaos in our family was now changing, as we rid ourselves of past suffering. Over and over again, others told me that it takes "time" to mend our lives, although that wasn't what I wanted to hear. Instead, I had to face the fact that my addiction had been raging for many years and my relationships were completely in shambles. We could not erase the pain overnight or in thirty days or in three months, but we could heal over "time." We were learning that recovery required a strong commitment from our entire family and not just me.

In recovery, I found that I don't have to prove anything to anyone. I am accountable only to God and to myself. Continuing to work daily on self-improvement is a struggle at times and, because I am human, I occasionally set myself up for disappointments. For example, when I make plans and also plan the outcome, the majority of times, the event doesn't turn out like I pictured it. As a result, I become disillusioned, with a tendency to become verbally self-destructive. It is best for me to avoid planning any results, so that I can bypass a lot of heartache and discouragement.

When things do not go well for me or I am physically tired, I am more vulnerable. It is during these periods that my destructive self-condemnation activates. During an aftercare meeting, one of the group members, Harold, confronted me about my habit of putting myself down. He disclosed, "You constantly degrade yourself with fatalistic statements. I think you need to change to more positive self-talk as soon as you hear your cynical self." After thinking about it, I knew he was right, so I agreed to be more aware of my self-criticism and attempted to reverse my messages.

After doing an awareness check for several days, I realized that I reproached myself most of the time and changing the habit was going to be tough. It was discouraging at first, because my corrections didn't happen fast enough. Rather than quit, as was my former custom, I had to keep reminding myself to practice patience and to work on myself until change occurred.

Throughout my recovery, I have come to understand that it is very easy to slip back into old destructive habits. Becoming dejected because of my impatience did nothing but set me up for further internal suffering. However, the payoffs of feeling good were worth going through the struggles. The only way for me to live without becoming overwhelmed with the unstable future was by practicing the AA philosophy, "one day at a time."

Although I have worked hard to change my negative messages to positive ones, I still slip back, and now and then berate myself for making a mistake. Whenever I do this, it helps to repeat several times, "I made a mistake and it's okay. I'll do better next time." What I'm doing is acknowledging my error and then reaffirming that it's okay not to be perfect. Rather than punishing myself further, the phrase, "I'll do better next time" (not perfect—but better), raises my low morale and reduces the emotional pressure. By practicing positive message reinforcement methods, I definitely improved my self-image.

This all sounds very simple, but it has been extremely difficult. Because I had heard negative, fatalistic messages since I was a toddler and throughout my adolescence, I believed them to be true. Then I supported those very same messages by repeating them to myself. In reality, I had been hearing derogatory messages from my parents or myself, nonstop, from childhood until I went into treatment. That was approximately thirty-nine years of believing that I am a worthless human being. No wonder I had so much trouble with change.

Being a perfectionist is an affliction that I have had to cope with all of my life, yet recognizing my habit has not been simple. During an aftercare meeting, Peter, one of the spouses, pointed out, "You put a tremendous burden on yourself by being such a perfectionist." I knew he was right. Here I was, trying to be the best aftercare group member ever. After the group discussed ways to deal with perfectionism, I picked up some valuable pointers. In order to avoid unnecessary pressure, I needed to reduce my expectations so that they were more realistic rather than unrealistic. By lowering my goals so I could reach them, I avoided setting myself up for disappointment. Whenever my goals are too high I tend to have a setback. The new insights were a start.

After several weeks of aftercare, one evening, insightful Harold blurted out a concern, "You know, John, I've noticed that you say 'you should' to your wife a lot." Somewhat surprised, John told the group he wasn't aware that he did this. As I thought about Harold's statement, I realized that throughout our married life, John had offered me his "you should" advice, which reminded me of my parents saying the same words to me when I was a child. Each time he said it, I would smolder inside. For years I had been storing up my feelings of resentment about my husband "shoulding" me. The time had come to deal with my feelings. Since most of the time John was unaware of his pattern, he asked the group and me to tell him whenever he slipped into his "should" mode.

I had frequent ups and downs the first years of my sobriety, which left me apprehensive about living in a world that had not reformed. In truth, I was afraid that I might want to drink again, which would result in a setback, as others had experienced before me. I had to face so many social pressures without alcohol that I wondered how I would cope. I remember attending my first social gathering with a group of John's business associates. Before going, I said to John, "Honey, I'm really scared about going to the party, where there's so much alcohol."

John was very supportive and suggested, "Why don't we make a plan? If you become nervous being around the drinking, just tell me and we can leave." Relieved, I accepted his offer and support, which gave me added strength. Throughout the evening, I kept a cola in my hand and stayed close to John. Fortunately, no one offered me a drink and after a few hours we left. Even though I had no desire to drink, it was a relief to be away from my enemy.

There were times when our children felt threatened as John and I began to break old patterns. In my drinking days, even though they protested, our children relied on John to handle their personal and emotional needs. However, in recovery they expressed mixed emotions about their desire to have John continue caretaking them. They didn't seem to appreciate the new quality of his interest in their lives, since he didn't have to center on me so much. More than they knew, our children had become used to their freedoms and they were not willing to let go of them easily. Now they were having to go to bed on time, do their homework at a specified hour, and follow through with their assigned household chores. The children weren't certain they liked the new corrections in our lives. Sometimes their distrust resulted in fighting, creating more difficulties that sabotaged our family recovery.

We found that doing the necessary personal work, which we had previously neglected, is really what recovery was all about. Each one in our family had an option to change. We could choose to recover or choose to relapse. However, if any of us reverted back to the former harmful behaviors, which we had relied upon when we were controlled by the disease, we wouldn't be successful. My counselor reminded the group frequently, "To put it simply, live your recovery program daily."

Searching for a balance in recovery has been complex at times. The many highs and lows in the first years of my sobriety created uncertainty for me. Sometimes I experienced a wonderful exhilaration; at other times I felt inadequate. I wondered, "When is my life going to even out? Why does recovery take so long?" There were no immediate answers.

Before we left treatment, our family was informed about Alcoholics Anonymous, (AA), an organization that was set up for the dependent person, and Alanon, the supportive organization for family members of chemically-addicted people. However, during our early period of recovery, we really didn't know how beneficial those self-help programs could be for our family. Sam advised me before I left treatment, "Your recovery will be much stronger and you will have a better chance if you became involved in AA." Although I wasn't too eager about the idea, I decided that my past judgments weren't very reliable, so why not give it a try?

Our family discovered that it was in AA and Alanon where the seed of recovery truly was cultivated. At the meetings, each person was nurtured by other dependents and co-dependents, who knew what we had been going through. I soon came to the conclusion that the people who founded the Alcoholics Anonymous program had established something quite extraordinary. The program really works for the millions of people who live the recovery steps in their search for sobriety. Who was I to come along and say, "I don't want to stay sober that way; I'll do my own program?" Many people have attempted to follow their own steps, but, sadly, the misguided ones who believe that they can revise the basic principles of AA have deluded themselves miserably and relapsed into using chemicals again.

Chapter Five of the AA Big Book, a guide for recovery, reminds members that many have unsuccessfully attempted to look for a simpler way to recovery. Several of my friends tried unsuccessfully to take a so-called "easier path." After relapsing a few times, some eventually discovered the hard way that the AA path *is* the easier way. Sadly, my treatment friend Mick struggled through a number of relapses with only brief periods of sobriety. Although he battled the disease in his "own way," he never truly surrendered to find the rewards of an AA recovery. Several years ago, this gentle man of many talents was found murdered, left amidst garbage in a dumpster in the slums of Seattle. Why he fought so hard against recovery, I could never understand. It is truly heart-breaking that there are many others, like Mick, who resist the program meant to save them from destruction.

I soon found out that the AA program is a program of discipline, and discipline wasn't one of my strong points. In the beginning, controlled by fear and mumbling and groaning about having to attend AA meetings, my body went but my heart did not. Once I was there, I attempted to be as invisible as I could manage. Hoping no one would ask me anything, I stuffed my fear aside and listened half-heartedly, anxious for the meeting to be over. After I unwillingly attended meetings for a few weeks and found that no demands were put upon me, I relaxed a bit. I found that I didn't have to be involved; others could do the talking.

Then, some weeks later, I realized that the people who weren't involved in the meetings didn't have the special glow of the ones who were dedicated to recovery. Whenever Mary Jane talked about her personal story, she had an inner, peaceful radiance with a contented presence about her that affected me deeply. I wanted what she had. Mary Jane told me many times, "Sobriety has to be your number one goal at all times." Her words made a big impact on me, giving a boost to my unsteady sobriety.

After I attended a number of meetings, I stopped worrying about what I was going to say. In my infancy in the program, I didn't truly understand what AA was really all about, but the wonderful thing about the program is that I didn't have to say anything if I didn't want to. In fact, my friend Resa told me, "When you are new in the AA program, you will learn far more by listening instead of trying to have all of the answers." That sounded good to me, since I was afraid to open my mouth. So I listened and I listened.

Something unusual happened to me each time I walked into an AA meeting. Eventually I experienced a sense of contentment, and I knew I was safe; I was where I belonged. Leaving my fears outside, an unexpected calmness would come over me. After the meeting, my spirits were usually high and I was ready to face whatever came before me, but not alone, for I always had the support of my AA friends.

At first, I was confused by all of the AA jargon and the clichés used at the meetings. Finally, as I quit resisting and thought the messages through, they became more clear. "Keep it simple," "This too will pass," "Let go, let God," "Easy does it," all meant just what they suggested. As I practiced the philosophies, I experienced the personal benefits that various members had talked about. What I heard at the meetings penetrated my soul, and recovery began to make sense. Each time I went to a meeting, I learned something new, which in turn helped my daily struggles to survive the illness.

When I didn't question or resist, the AA teachings were simple. I was determined that no matter how difficult a time I had or what obstacles I needed to overcome, I was going the follow the AA program to recovery. And I did. Everything has worked exactly like Alcoholics Anonymous said it would.

In AA I found what I was looking for—internal peace, happiness, joy, self-acceptance. I began to realize that my sobriety was a priceless gift, not to be taken for granted. The caliber of my sobriety depended on the energy I was willing to put into it. AA offered me an incredible journey of love without judgments, along with freedom from my addiction. I don't want to ever lose what I have found in this wonderful organization; it means my life to me.

Finding a sponsor in AA, someone who I could relate to and who had a strong personal recovery was a tremendous help to me. I was impressed with the quality of sobriety that Mary Jane had. When I first met her, she had been sober for fourteen years. I figured she must know something, so I asked her if she would be my sponsor. She agreed and has been a great inspiration to me ever since. At times I didn't like what she told me, but she was wise in the ways of the disease, as well as in the ways of recovery.

A few weeks after our first meeting, I told Mary Jane, "I have trouble focusing on just today. My fear gets in the way, and I end up worrying about the future. Can I stay sober for forty more years?"

Mary Jane tried to reassure me, "It helps when you tell yourself that today is all you have, over and over." She acknowledged that at times practicing the philosophies of my new life would be hard. Then she asked, "Has anyone ever indicated to you that recovery would be easy?"

With some hesitation, I replied, "No, not really. I had only hoped it would be." There I was—doing one of my old trips, worrying about things that hadn't happened and setting myself up for defeat.

She replied, "One thing that will help you focus on just one day at a time is taking a daily inventory." I had heard that a daily inventory, a time to check out progress at the end of each day, was an important tool for monitoring recovery. As I thought about the value of this and tried it out, I decided that I had no reason to continue making my life miserable by worrying about events and people over which I had no control. Perhaps if I learned to quit fighting life and let go, I would have fewer problems.

In aftercare, my counselor suggested, "Joann, you need to take a look at how controlling you are." Instantly my denial activated as I prepared to defend myself. When Sam explained that it didn't mean I had something wrong with me, I took a deep breath, relaxed my defenses, and thought about his statement. I had been taking everyone's problems on as my problems, supervising situations that were not my concern. Often I tried to control my husband or my children by directing them in some way. Learning that it was not my job to keep things in perfect order has been a battle.

Even so, I still have problems trying to govern certain things in my life. For example, allowing my husband to drive without my help is one control area that I have a problem eliminating. I don't know how he manages without me to help him find his way about town, but he does. Closing my eyes, biting my tongue, and telling myself that it is his problem if he gets lost is probably the only way for me to stop.

It helps to remind myself each day that the only person I really have control over is me. Whether I go to AA meetings or attend weekly therapy sessions, the important thing is totally committing myself. If my sobriety is my number one priority, I can't afford to allow other events to interfere with my program of recovery. Anytime I start making excuses and concessions that are in conflict with my commitment to my recovery, I am in trouble.

During the first months of aftercare, a couple of people from other groups relapsed. It really concerned me, so one evening I said to my group, "When my friends relapse, it really scares me. They appeared to be doing fine; what went wrong?" No one was certain about the cause, but the group believed complacency might have been a major factor. Becoming complacent about my recovery and my disease was a trap I had been warned about. Though I had stopped the spread of the disease, I knew it would never entirely go away.

If I believe that my sobriety is absolutely safe, that I have control over my disease and I don't need meetings, these are signs that I am setting myself up for a relapse. I mustn't ignore the warnings that the powerful disease will never stop trying to seduce me into relapse. I know that if I drink again, the disease will take over immediately, guiding me toward the road of destruction.

Certainly, many people exist who have abstained from alcohol and who are not involved in AA. Sometimes I wondered, "Are they dry or are they sober?" There is a definite difference between the two. I remember Drake, who relapsed at least five times. Even though the drugs were gone, he was still belligerent, the same as when he used chemicals. One day Leita, his wife and my friend, told me, "You know, the family believes that Drake was easier to get along with and less threatening when he was under the influence of drugs than when he was 'dry' and hostile." She was afraid that Drake never understood that it wasn't enough to stop drugs without changing behaviors. She was right. His behavior became worse and, after relapsing the fifth time, while drunk, he ran his car into a brick wall, killing himself. The disease had claimed another victim.

Drake's death made a big impact on me, reinforcing my personal commitment. There was no way I wanted to end up being another statistic of the disease, so I strengthened my program. Then another door in my recovery opened as I found my way to the state AA convention held in Eugene, Oregon, called Summerfest. Mary Jane told me, "It's a wonderful experience. Over a thousand recovering dependents and co-dependents are going to be there." When she said that, my heart plummeted. It was hard to say no to Mary Jane, so I overcame my fear of large crowds and attended the conference. She was right about there being a lot of people, but the experience was a peak one. I don't believe I've ever been in the company of so many happy people, filled with love. The conference room and halls were bursting with such a commanding excitement and healing that I got goose bumps. The power that was present was so uplifting that my personal resolutions were reinforced.

There is a saying in AA, "You can't keep it if you don't give it away." Although I had heard this statement before, I wasn't sure what it really meant until my experience at Summerfest. I realized that I was witnessing the ultimate demonstration of "giving it away." The thousand or more people giving their experience of hope and love to others was what it was all about.

There was no doubt at times that I set obstacles in my path of recovery. Sometimes I gave myself excuses to refrain from taking on new challenges. For instance, when my son Don began to teach me the basics of operating a computer, I felt completely overwhelmed. By telling myself that it was because I was stupid and unable to comprehend this complicated operation, I gave myself an excuse to give up. However, I counteracted those defeating messages and gave myself some encouragement. Today, I actually enjoy my computer rather than call it names, at least most of the time.

Fear that I won't live up to the expectations of myself and others often gets in the way of my progress. Letting go of my guilt and forgiving myself for not being perfect has been hard to practice. However, through time and pain, my recovery eventually stabilized. As I matured emotionally and became secure in recovery, I didn't have to run to Serenity Lane, and Sam, for answers to every problem. As I worked through issues, my personal well-being increased, allowing me to understand myself more clearly. As much as

I wanted complete recovery right now, I knew deep inside that repairing the destruction of the disease would require a lifetime.

Asking for help was not easy for me. Reaching out to Sam, to my friends in treatment, or to my AA friends saved me countless times. However, I knew that depending on them too much wasn't healthy either. I had to find a balance. I avoided a lot of heartache and disappointment by tucking my pride away and saying, "I need help." My requests for assistance were never turned down. Over the years, my friends were there, guiding me along the path of recovery. My heart is full of gratitude for their endless patience and love. My thanks to the many people who have touched my life can never repay the benefits I have gained.

My search for peace did not end the day I left treatment, nor did it culminate the day following my abstinence from alcohol. Peace and happiness happened gradually as I developed my new lifestyle. Today my life is full of happiness. Countless rewards come each day that I never dreamed would be mine, and the beauty of it is, my life continues to be filled with the peace I wanted for so long. I know for certain that God led this resisting person, through others, to the doors of Serenity Lane. I was shown the reality of divine love, for which I am eternally grateful. God's purpose for me is still unfolding to this day, behind the words on these pages, letting others know there is hope for us all.

For many years I thought God didn't hear me, but I was wrong. My words were heard, but the answers were different than I had anticipated. Today I am not so impatient (at least most of the time), and I wait until God shows me the way. Instead of trying to control my destiny to my liking, I am able to let life happen.

At the beginning of my recovery from this devastating disease, I knew I owed my life to Sam, who helped me come back from the depths of hell to a life more fulfilling and happy than I could ever have imagined. He was gentle and insightful, caring yet demanding, and he assisted me with vision into myself, the positive as well as the negative parts. He helped me love myself and care about living. He made me cry, he made me angry, he made me love again, he nurtured me and tended my wounds. He helped me care about others and accepted me for myself, as he gave me hope for a new life. He gave me new meaning for being, letting me know that my feelings were okay, helping me share them, learn about them, and not feel guilty about them. Through all of the pain, he gave me guidance and courage to accept new challenges, as he brought me back to the love and care of my lost friend, God, all of which I am eternally grateful for. He gave me far more than mere words and thanks can ever express.

Five years after my treatment, this special man joined our family. His beautiful daughter married my handsome son. Together, they have presented to us three wonderful grandchildren to share with Grandpa Sam and Grandma Vivian.

10

FOLLOWING THROUGH

THE SOCIAL SCENE gave me the greatest problem in my recovery. It wasn't that I wanted to drink; it was a problem just being in a situation where there was so much alcohol available. One party we attended early in my recovery was a real test for me. Like all cocktail parties, everyone stood around talking about nothing and smiling, pretending to enjoy themselves. An associate of John's, Terry, kept himself busy circulating from group to group, then stopped near me. Hovering nervously, he waited to join in, then he noticed that I was drinking a cola, so, winking knowingly at me, he offered to get me a "real" drink. Trying to discourage him, I told him that I was fine, but the little pest of a man persisted. Again and again he tried to talk me into a more "potent" drink. After Terry's fourth attempt to persuade me, I told him outright, "I really can't drink because I am an alcoholic." Mischievously I added, "And alcohol makes me really sick, so I lose complete control and attack people, start breaking furniture and windows, and the police usually have to haul me off to jail." Looking in his face innocently, I continued, "And if that happened, then you would be responsible, since you wanted me to drink."

With his mouth agape, the man with the small brain said no more and he ran out of the room as fast as his short little legs would carry him.

In all the years of recovery, that was the only time that I recall anyone attempting to push a drink on me. As a rule, most of the people I know are aware that I am recovering and they are respectful of my sobriety. Even the drinkers know, so of course they keep their distance when we are together in a social situation. My presence actually makes them uncomfortable and sometimes ruins their drinking for them. In any event, I need to be aware at all times that alcohol is a powerful drug and that my disease of alcoholism is completely deceptive. When I am susceptible and least expect it, the disease wants to tempt me, reminding me of its many rewards, of how it can provide pleasure to my unsuspecting body and mind. Very often, the subtle seduction happens through other people, like Terry, who want me to know what fun I am missing.

Even though going to social drinking occasions is uncomfortable for me, on the other hand, isolation from others is even more destructive. If I refrain from being involved in social or work groups, I prevent the development of my confidence and self-worth. In the past, there were many times when I felt socially inadequate. At the same time, if I didn't become involved with others, it gave me an excuse to avoid any kind of competition or challenge. It is too risky for me to isolate myself in recovery, for without involvement it is unlikely that I will be successful.

There were times in the past when I wanted to achieve a particular goal, but wasn't certain how to do it. For instance, some years ago, I was interested in taking a cake decorating class. I have had some talent in this art form ever since I tried to disguise my first half-inch disaster as a young bride. Since then I made and decorated cakes for every occasion in our family. However, I had to drive Renae and Lorene to and from school each day, which took a lot of time out of each day. Between the children and my duties at home and at John's business, I felt I couldn't even consider asking my husband if I could take the class, so I didn't bring it up. At that point in my life, letting go of another goal wasn't anything new. More often than not I used the family as an excuse to avoid pursuing my interests. The truth was, I just didn't have the courage to emerge from my protective shell of insecurity.

In other instances, I did attempt to communicate verbally what I wanted, but I wasn't heard, or I didn't know how to express my desires clearly. In my attempt to advance my goals, I resorted to various methods, one being manipulation, to fulfill my needs.

One time stands out for me, when I was completely unaware that I was manipulating the situation. I wanted to go out to dinner, but was afraid to ask John to take me. One evening when he was in a mellow mood, I finally developed enough courage to tell him about a popular restaurant. I informed him, "My friend Sylvia and her husband ate at this fantastic restaurant. They had a marvelous time and the food was excellent." My hope was that John would say, "Sounds great, would you like to go there for dinner, too?" I visualized myself in a lovely, romantic setting. My thoughtful husband sat by my side, looking lovingly at me in my new dress. In front of me was an outstanding meal, awaiting my pleasure. The picture was well formed in my mind, since I had been thinking about it for several days.

I waited for his delighted response. Nothing happened. He was reading the paper, so I thought, "Maybe he didn't hear me." I repeated my information. After a lengthy pause he said, "That's nice," and continued to read his paper, not knowing he had disappointed me.

What I had done was set myself up to be disenchanted by not being direct with him. A better approach would have been to ask him openly, "John, I would like to have dinner at this marvelous restaurant where Sylvia and her husband ate at last week. Shall we go tonight?" First of all, I would have been direct, and secondly, I would have stated what I wanted. These are two very key elements for good communication skills that I was unaware of at the time. When I manipulated (the first example), any number of answers were possible, such as, "I'm glad they enjoyed themselves," or "I don't like that type of restaurant," or "Why don't you go with them next time?" So the chances of getting what I wanted by manipulation were not good at all. Whereas, if I had asked him directly (example two), I had a 50% chance of getting what I wanted. He could either say "No," or "Yes."

In recovery, I found that playing games was really not worth the price, that it is far more healthy to have good communication practices. As a general rule, when I am fair with others, they are fair with me. When I am honest with others, they will usually be honest with me. In any event, my needs won't be met by being dishonest with myself and other people.

Whenever my goals are too far reaching and impossible to achieve, excessive tension builds up inside me. In order to avoid adding more pressure than I am able to handle, I must make certain that my goals are realistic. For example, if I have a stressful day I find that physical exercise of some kind helps me reduce the stress. Walking, running, tennis, or bicycling are activities that help decrease my tensions and clear my mind so that I am able to function more effectively. Music is another helpful, relaxing therapy that I often use. Gentle, soothing background music facilitates more efficient work at my office or home.

By deep breathing, that is, inhaling and exhaling deeply in a slow, even rhythm, for about three minutes, I am able to cope better with anxiety-building situations. Having a good support system of friends, with whom I can talk openly and honestly about my stress, helps me a lot. My biggest obstacle is reaching out to them and admitting that I need help. Not only is it crucial for me to discuss problems with my faithful supporters, but I need to be open to their advice on how to reduce certain stressful situations.

Checking out my diet regularly is imperative to my stress reduction. Am I skipping meals or eating foods/drink which create hypertension? Alcoholics have a physical imbalance that doesn't tolerate any kind of mood-altering substance, including too much caffeine, sugar, or chocolate. These are ingredients that produce anxiety or jitters and sometimes loss of sleep for me. Today, I know that eating balanced meals consistently not only benefits me physically, but mentally as well. Even so, sometimes I give in to the call of the "Peanut Buster Parfait," and then must pay the price for my impulsive indulgence.

When I am hurting, I search for ways to stop the hurt. If I choose an inappropriate method to reduce pain, such as food, I may get a temporary sense of well-being, but overindulging in food inevitably leads to guilt. The end result is that my self-image deteriorates. Each time I am tempted, I remember the comfort food offers.

It is clear to me now that any addiction will destroy me, whether it is alcohol, drugs, food, work, or gambling. I was harmed emotionally, physically, mentally, and spiritually by my compulsive addiction to alcohol. It drove me, controlled me, and eventually the disease became my master, and yet, I never started out with the intention of becoming addicted. I only became involved with alcohol because it made me feel better. With cunning skill it gave me a reward, a happiness, a personal sense of well-being that fed my fragile ego. As a result, I desired more, wanting to recapture the same rewards it gave me initially. It is critical for me to be constantly vigilant to my susceptibility to addiction.

Adequate rest is also necessary for me in developing a healthy attitude about myself and life in general. It helps me to be much more productive and happier with myself, but if I am not providing myself with enough sleep hours, then I become crabby and negative. It is essential to eliminate unnecessary projects if my life is so full of activities that I don't have time to sit and relax. Overdoing has been an old habit that I have to watch carefully in my recovery.

If my stomach is tight and my muscles and jaw are tense, it is usually a sign that I am not working through my emotions or that I am worrying over things I cannot change. Some people laugh a lot when they are stressed out, others have problems overeating, or not eating at all. When I am under a great deal of emotional pressure, I become irritable, generating a critical and defensive attitude. In the past, sometimes I attempted to run away from problems, and at other times I cried in complete frustration. This had to change in recovery. I couldn't run from my problems anymore.

It is vital for me to continue learning about healthy ways to handle my stress and not permit it to accumulate. If I allow stress buildup, I am not taking care of myself appropriately. Tending to my health includes processing my problems effectively and consistently in order to help me avoid inner conflict. I cannot afford to become preoccupied with other things, overlooking the dangers which threaten my sobriety. When I make a list at the end of the day, regarding what I did and said throughout the day, it helps me see the areas that get me into trouble.

A key discovery I made in recovery is that the negative feelings, which I had stuffed inside of myself throughout my drinking years, were a primary reason for so many of my physical problems. Consequently, the more feelings I ignored, the more my body suffered. Not only that, but my emotional problems definitely increased. Looking back, I can see that I financially supported many of the doctors in our city.

During early recovery, I became aware that all human beings experience the same feelings. For me, learning to process those feelings was one of the most demanding tasks to undertake. I had to continually remind myself that if I suppressed my feelings, denying their importance, they would come out in some other way. For example, if I blocked my anger, my childhood message, "Little girls don't get angry," would get in the way, but nevertheless the anger got expressed. I just used verbal abuse as my weapon of choice. When I avoided dealing with my angry feelings, my resentments ended up controlling me. In the end, I would find myself thinking about my bitterness obsessively, figuring out ways to get even.

Another area I learned about in recovery was grief. Most of us have grief issues that are not totally settled. Some, like me, used alcohol/drugs to numb the emotional pain from past, unresolved grief issues. Others sometimes suppress their grief or anger at a person indefinitely. Whenever there is a death of anyone, we experience a variety of emotions such as anger, hurt, fear, and loneliness. This assortment of feelings remains unresolved if we have inadequate skills to deal with them.

The friendships that I developed in treatment are life-long and their love will never be forgotten. One friend in particular, Webb, was a source of strength for me. All through the years of sobriety we kept in touch, helping each other through struggles, trying to find the balance in a healthy recovery. His sudden death left much sorrow in my heart. It was difficult for me to deal with this painful loss, so I wrote him a letter, wanting to let him know how much he meant to me.

I wrote:

To my friend Webb,
There is no question you will be greatly missed in my life. How can I ever fill the void you have left? We have been through so much, coming far down the road of life, recovering from our disease, sharing and listening to each other. The support you gave me through the past 16-1/2 yrs. we

have known each other, can never be measured. I will never forget you were there when I needed to talk, helping me see what was before me, supporting me without judgment.

I will remember you as a gentleman who never let me pay for my lunch, or your lunch even when it was your birthday. You were always kind to put up with my lectures about killing yourself with cigarettes (reformed smokers can be such a pain, can't they?), never telling me to mind my own business, but knowing in your heart I wanted you to stay around a bit longer, and that I cared what happened. You knew I was scared for you, but you kept your own fears to yourself. Throughout the painful years, you never let your wonderful sense of humor get away from you, no matter how bad things were.

My friend, you were so brave about your pain, never complaining or blaming, even though you had given up the fight. I'm glad you allowed God's love to touch your heart and soul. I'm happy you found God's strength could be your strength. You are in good hands, and your pain is no more. You have at last found complete peace.

Webb, I'm grateful for your strong influence on me. I want to thank you for touching my life, for being my friend. Life won't be quite the same without you. The emptiness will take a long time to heal, but I wanted you to know your love and support changed me in many ways. I thank God for giving me such a special and rare friend as you. It was a blessing for us both.

Love, your friend,
Joann

Through the pain and tears, I was able to start my grief-healing process by writing this letter. As I worked through my emotions, I began to let go, acknowledging my loss. My only regret is that I never actually said all of those words to Webb before he died. Even though our friendship meant a lot to us, and we both knew it in our hearts, I still wish I had expressed these words while he was alive. It has taught me to pay closer attention to talking about my thoughts and feelings with my friends and family while they are still with me.

Grief is not always associated with the death of a person. There may be deep sadness surrounding a job change, or we might have grief concerning moving from our home or city. Whatever the reason, those painful emotions need to be talked about. Getting involved in grief therapy is an excellent method for many to help process their emotional trauma, or going to a private therapist is another way to work through these difficult periods of life.

Whenever I am going through a grieving time, I tend to suppress my anger or hurt because it is too upsetting to think about. Through my drinking years, I grieved about my miserable marriage and unhappy life. I ran away from my grief, drowning my inadequate role as a parent by drinking. Although I didn't know it, I was grieving the loss of what I had never had in a healthy relationship with my family. The alcohol blocked my feelings, so I didn't have to hurt or think about what was underneath the pain. Recovery helped me understand that no matter what I feel, the feelings are real and they are my personal emotions. I have a right to every one of them. The problem occurs when I attempt to suppress the feelings and pretend they don't exist.

At the time I didn't realize it, but when I went into treatment, I grieved over the loss of my friend alcohol. It had been my close ally for years, and now that relationship was ended. Alcohol could no longer be my medication. I couldn't depend on it to salve my wounds, so I had to move beyond the grief, through the emotions, to the other side.

When my father died, at first I didn't think I had any feelings about it since we were not close. However, I soon learned that there were feelings waiting to surface. My first feeling was shock, then I experienced some relief that I didn't have to experience his rejection any longer. After that, I went through sadness concerning so much that we missed out on in a father/daughter relationship. Underneath it all was a great deal of hurt and loneliness, which was not easy for me to acknowledge. The pain of loss for something we never had, that we could never experience in the future, stayed with me until I eventually worked through my feelings.

In all matters of grief my body is affected, causing me to have difficulty sleeping or eating. Sometimes I felt the sensation of tightness in my chest; other times it felt like someone had punched me in the stomach. There have been moments when I would suddenly break out crying at the realization of the trauma I was going through.

After our fox terrier, Tami, died a senseless and brutal death a couple of years after I completed treatment, I grieved. She had been with our family since she was a puppy. While I was at work, John came home for lunch and found Tami lying dead on the driveway, with her belly skin sliced open in a rectangular shape, leaving her organs exposed. No natural accident could cause her terrible death, so it was determined that someone, possibly in a cult, had deliberately done this horrible act at another location. Somehow Tami got home, but she died from exposure and shock. We just couldn't believe that anyone could act so viciously, especially toward a defenseless animal. Our family grieved over Tami's murder for a long time, for she was loved and part of our family.

Although grieving is a painful process for me, I must go through the various steps at my own rate and not suppress my emotions indefinitely. The grieving is not finished in a matter of minutes or hours but often takes me a long time to resolve. In any case, it is vital for me to talk about my grief with close friends so that I am able to receive significant relief. If I think my grief feelings will go away by themselves in time, I merely bury them further inside by not taking care of them. The times when I have unexpectedly come in touch with some past neglected grief are important reminders that I must take care of all of my personal grieving in the moment I become aware of it.

A particularly difficult area for me to examine was my grief concerning the pain I put my children through. The drinking years prevented John and me from understanding what they were experiencing. However, during recovery, as I realized that our children had suppressed their emotional pain throughout their young lives, my grief became more acute. As I dealt with my grief over so much loss during this time, our family developed new understanding and concern for each other. As I turned my life around, I became committed to expressing my love more openly and frequently to my family.

It is a tragedy that during the fundamental period of parenting we wasted so much time in conflict and suffering. If I had known what "compromise" meant, I could have taught it to our children. Perhaps life would have been less complicated for us all. If I had had the skill of mentally changing places with the children, and they with me, we might have understood each other better. Maybe our visions wouldn't have been so limited if we had each taken care of our personal responsibilities and respected each other's individual space. More family harmony would have been possible by communicating openly with each other, by verbalizing feelings, and by praising and talking about concerns on a regular basis. The doors between our family could have opened in ways that none of us thought possible so that we might gain peace and unity. However, this did not happen for us. Instead, in our blindness, we missed the possibilities for more positive relationships with each other. For lack of knowledge, we lost so much. When I think back, I find it truly amazing that our family survived this painful period of our lives at all.

One thing that helped me through this unsettled time was to pray for patience and the ability to keep my sanity.

*John and
Joann during
their visit to
the beach*

*John and Joann
camping in the
mountains*

*John and
Joann boating
at the lake*

There is a saying in AA that I wished I had known about when raising our adolescents, "This too shall pass." I could have reassured myself countless times with those words of reminder.

Many obstacles can hinder my personal growth, but so often I don't know what they are. Whenever I am too intense my sense of values is disturbed and along with it my lighter, more humorous side. At these times, I forget how to laugh at myself or be happy with my attainments. Nonetheless, it is crucial to take an honest look at all areas as soon as I am conscious of them. If I find that any one of them is a problem for me, and is obstructing my self-growth, my course must change in order to avoid serious problems.

Though times were much better in recovery, my family still had doubts. John asked himself, "How do I trust myself to love again after living with an alcoholic wife for so long?" The children wondered, "How do we deal with our fear if we see Mom's old behaviors return?" Before long, the doubts dwindled away as we learned how to practice self-care. I had to earn my family's trust through my example of healthy growth. Only then could we see our faith and hope in each other gradually being restored.

The damage resulting from my past negative actions has taken years to identify and correct. Our children carried the scars of living in a chemical family with them when they left home as adults. They had no healthy examples to draw on, so they didn't know how to feel good about themselves. It follows that their personal relationships with loved ones and friends were affected by our traumatic past. Since our children lived in a dysfunctional home for such a long time, they found it difficult to trust and give love in other meaningful relationships.

Today our children have obtained education about the effects of the disease on families, and they have become aware that they have more personal work to do in healing those complex wounds. Our family has worked hard to deal

*John and Joann
after a game of
tennis*

*John after a
vigorous
tennis match*

with the buried sorrows, to overcome the restraints that kept each one of us locked into our disease. We are becoming a healthy family, each learning what a strong relationship consists of. It is remarkable that our children, despite their past obstacles, have developed into the loving adults and parents they are today.

Regretfully, it has taken me far too long to fully understand that our children are God's most precious gifts, entrusted to John and me to nurture, to love, and to guide. Even with all of the pain we lived through, we are blessed to have learned from our mistakes, and to have discovered love and hope for a better life.

Although the healing is taking place every moment of our lives, I will never forget the despair, the emotional pain, the ongoing misery, that our family lived for so long. The painful reminders keep me working on myself and my progress. Even though at times I revert back to my old habits, for the most part my focus remains on the present. It's the only way I can live.

John and I didn't know how to be close or intimate at the beginning of recovery. Alcoholism controlled us for so long that all we knew was loneliness and hurt. Though our life was unstable at this time, John's trust returned, allowing us hope that things would improve. We didn't have to wait any longer for a "miracle" to happen; instead we took the initiative to make our own miracle happen. In so doing, what we had always wanted for ourselves became a certainty.

Putting our lives together again has taken constant daily vigilance. Even though progress has been slower than I like, the rewards have been immeasurable. Through numerous struggles, our love has been completely renewed. Now it is a stronger, more sensitive and beautiful love than we experienced in the past. John and I have become best friends, caring deeply for one another, sharing countless joys. Discovering the pure enjoyment of unconditional love has brought new meaning into our lives. Just being in each

John and Joann at annual family costume party

Joann's surprise birthday party

other's company is a special time of genuine happiness that we both cherish very much. Looking forward to being with each other as much as possible is a joy that grows through our years together. The contentment that we feel, whether it be holding hands, hugging, or snuggling at night, satisfies us completely. Our bonding and pure love is a genuine miracle.

Not every family is blessed, as our family was, to get help before being completely destroyed. It is sad that so many families wait far too long before they seek help, and when they finally do, most are unwilling to invest the time and work it takes to rebuild the family unit again. Sure, it takes time, constant work, sacrifice, honesty, compromise, and willingness to change. But whatever we want in life that is worthwhile takes all of this and much more, and in recovery it is all worth our complete commitment. For families to come back from death and destruction is no small feat, so I feel extremely grateful to God for helping us find family recovery.

Part Two

Joann and some of her bear friends

11

INNER PEACE— SPIRITUAL PEACE

WHILE I WAS IN TREATMENT, a nun named Sister Martha visited from California and lectured to the patients and staff at Serenity Lane. I will never forget this wonderful lady, or the impact she had on my life. It was as if God's spirit radiated from within her. As I observed this holy woman interacting with patients and staff, I was profoundly moved. She exuded a powerful spiritual essence, unlike anything I had ever witnessed before.

When she spoke, her words were full of the loving gentleness of Jesus. As she talked about Jesus's love, I could feel a compassionate love enclose the room. On one occasion, she lightly touched my shoulder as she walked by. My entire body tingled, as if an electric shock had jolted through me, followed by an inner calmness. One of the thoughts she shared that made a strong impression on me was, "God loves us very much and when we stray from God's path we are given spankings, but when we follow in God's footsteps we are rewarded." I thought to myself, "No wonder I've been hurting so much; God has been spanking me for a long time."

Almost immediately, my inner vision cleared. Looking at the many experiences that had happened to me lately— treatment, direction from an insightful counselor and group, AA inspirations, my chaplain's spiritual guidance, and my family's continuing support, were all significant influences that I couldn't ignore. Now, unexpectedly, this nun came into my life like a brilliant light, leading me further away from the past darkness. I realized that everything that had recently occurred was guiding me back toward God. It was at this point that I decided to get "on the path" and find a way to improve my life. After making my critical decision, I was overcome with a complete sense of serenity. Perhaps I would be able to discover some of the rewards the spiritual woman was talking about, after all.

Another thought she shared was, "Flowers are God's gift to us, a way of telling us God loves us." Those simple words were beautiful and absolutely true. Since that time, whenever I look at flowers I think of those words and that special woman. It is true that every flower has its own distinct beauty, just as every human being has a unique individuality. Nevertheless, if the flowers around us aren't lovingly attended to, they will wither and die. Flowers, as well as people, need nourishment to help them thrive, to help them become strong and to bloom. Without nurturing, our lives become meaningless.

I wanted to talk to Sister Martha and ask her, "Please tell me what to do," but the words wouldn't come. Perhaps she saw the look of desperation in my eyes, prompting her touch of peace. I often wonder what would have happened to me if I had not had the "opportunity" to hear the special message of God sent through this extraordinary nun. Once a year she traveled through Eugene, spending at least one day with the patients and staff at "The Lane." For me to be in treatment at the time she spoke to the patients is "one of those amazing coincidences" that we talk about in recovery.

Before entering treatment, most of the time I struggled and fought against life in my search for inner peace. Now this lady, with the mere touch of her hand, made me feel peace throughout my entire being. To me, inner peace really means spiritual peace—they are one and the same. Although I had searched for true peace since childhood, now I could finally feel it. There was nothing quite like it.

As I thought about my search for internal peace, I realized that it began long ago, when I was a child. Since I was raised in the Catholic faith, I was instructed that spirituality was a special gift. I was taught that those who practiced their faith and disciplined their lives would eventually find spiritual peace. Although I believed in my faith and felt close to God at times, inner peace seemed to elude me. The Catholic faith required members to be disciplined in everything. Besides being expected to attend church each Sunday and go to Catholic school, I was encouraged to make personal sacrifices—such as no meat on Fridays and giving up sweets during Advent and Lent, the preparation times for major religious events. For years, I went without in order to strengthen my individual character on my way to gaining spiritual peace.

During my school years and into my marriage, I practiced my faith diligently, searching for my promised tranquility. However, it still evaded me, so I assumed I wasn't trying hard enough. John and I raised our three children in the same faith in which we grew up, but still my search remained unfulfilled. Later on, as our family dissension developed and multiplied, my faith began to suffer and vanished almost completely. I became angry and blamed God, who had previously been my friend. Unhappiness and disappointments distorted my once strong belief in my faith. As my life filled with misery, my spiritual concepts became confused. I felt completely abandoned. With a twisted outlook, I told my family, "We're put on earth to suffer, until we completely fall apart." During this painful time, I believed that I wasn't meant to have any true happiness or peace—that it was my destiny to be wretched.

As my bitterness toward my faith and God grew, so did my alcoholism. I felt that I had been lied to by the entire Church and anyone connected with it. Resentful, I reminded myself, "They promised me peace, yet there was never any peace for me." Nevertheless, I was afraid that if I verbalized my anger I would be punished further, so I suppressed it, allowing it to control me for years. By the time I entered the doors of the treatment center, I was filled with antagonism. Not only was I angry at God, but also at my entire family and the world. In my tormented mind, I believed that they were responsible for my life of turmoil, and this kept me from finding peace. Being forced into treatment, I concluded, was my ultimate punishment for being a "bad" person.

Even though it wasn't pleasant, looking into the windows of my past at the desolate emptiness of my life, now I could finally see the light at the end of the tunnel. My painful self-analyzing was really the start of my spiritual recovery. Now I realized that it was me who had strayed off the path, by giving up my search for peace. It wasn't God who had abandoned me; instead it was I who had abandoned God.

In AA there is emphasis on what is called "a spiritual awakening," and I realized that my spirit was now coming alive. By all logic, I should have been dead from years of alcohol abuse, but through a miracle I had been spared from certain self-destruction by the reprieve of treatment. Just when I thought I was spiritually dead, my heart and soul opened in that moment when Sister Martha touched my shoulder. I could see that my drinking and self-preoccupation had made me blind to God's watchful presence at every turn of my life. In order to have peace within myself, I needed to be at peace with God. I had carelessly mislaid my faith for a period of time; now it gave me great peace to have found it again.

Each day in treatment I prayed for direction, "Please God, show me the way." Inside, I wondered if perhaps there was something else I was meant to do. As I contemplated my future direction, I found inner peace in other areas besides my faith. In addition to the gift of spiritual life, God gave me another opportunity with my family. Making amends to them brought each of us a stronger love, along with peace and contentment. As I became more reliable in my responsibilities as a wife and mother, I felt much more tranquility. Although my family and working my program took most of my time, I felt strongly about wanting to do something more with my life.

My desire to help others first came to me in treatment and has been a major part of my life since that time. Filled with gratitude, I turned my life over to God, asking what I could do in return. Shortly after that, nurse Mary Ann asked me, "Would you be interested in training to be a nurse's aide?" Now I knew in my heart what God had in mind for me. Since then, I have contributed my services to Serenity Lane for many years, which has given me a great deal of peace. It has been my way of saying thanks for another chance. Although I don't believe that I can totally give back what I have gained, I will continue helping as long as I can.

Occasions always arise to help another prisoner of the disease of addiction. The many individual rewards of peace, joy, and satisfaction that I receive from my work outweigh any reimbursement. I experience a wonderful excitement at seeing families with new hope take hold of recovery, then change before my eyes. When a person filled with years of pain begins to share their most intimate thoughts and feelings, which have been locked inside them, I am moved beyond words. Being a part of the miracle of mending lives truly heals my soul.

As my personal and spiritual growth developed, I tried new challenges, things that I would never have dreamed of attempting before treatment. For instance, one of the new peaceful pleasures I discovered was oil painting. Following my discharge from treatment, my son Don asked me, "Mom, would you like to take my place in an oil painting class? I can't take the class now because of my university enrollment." I thought about it and agreed to give it a try.

Painting was a long hidden desire that I never had the courage to attempt, and since sobriety, my hands weren't shaking anymore. Even though I first attended the class with the unrealistic idea that I could become a Rembrandt, I had a great time anyway. I found out painting is not only fun, but fulfilling, and a surprisingly peaceful experience. Now I spend many relaxing hours sitting in front of my canvas, with my absorption so complete that it seems like only minutes have passed. Although I'm still not a Rembrandt, I discovered that I have some talent, and I learn new skills with each painting. What really matters was that I took a risk and attempted a creative venture.

John was also searching for peace within himself. While trying to please everyone around him for such a long time, he had created internal chaos for himself. During aftercare he realized that he had to address his own problems. At one of our aftercare meetings, good old Harold confronted him, "It seems like you're always being the 'good guy' John, and available for everyone to lean on." John agreed he had trouble with this, and over time he had forgotten how to say "no" to the demands of others. He told the group he would work on taking care of himself first, rather than last, but it hasn't been easy.

Another area that interfered with his own search for peace was trying to direct my recovery. One of John's beliefs was that in order for me to feel good inside, I needed to be busy, so that I wouldn't be tempted to drink again. However, his idea of finding peace was somewhat different than mine. Among the many activities on our new agenda was taking tennis lessons together. Of course my typical unrealistic expectations of playing like Chris Evert, the famous tennis champion, the first time I set foot on the court, nearly did me in. As I stumbled around the court, chasing the fuzzy yellow ball while attempting to hit it with my racket, I kept telling myself, "This is fun." I wasn't sure if it was a statement or a question. When my muscles ached from being reactivated after years of alcohol saturation, I said, "This is good for you." Despite setting myself up with unreasonable expectations at the beginning of my lessons, I eventually became more realistic.

Through the years of romancing and pursuing this small, yet frequently elusive ball, I found that tennis is truly a fun sport. Now I am able to hit the ball with my racket more than miss it. That's not perfection, but it's progress. The ball even goes in the direction I intend, at least most of the time. Like any sport, on occasion it's rewarding, then at other times it's highly frustrating. However, it's what I put into my efforts that makes it worthwhile. If I am continually down on myself, I don't do well. In contrast, if I am supportive and give myself positive messages, my performance will be far more productive. I must admit, in the beginning weeks, tennis offered me very little peace. Instead, it gave me lots of frustration. However, as I mastered the game, I relaxed more and felt really good about myself.

The pleasure I experience after attempting and accomplishing new endeavors not only increases my personal growth, but it also gives me internal harmony. To know I can risk stepping out of my individual boundaries in order to broaden my perspectives is a sign that I'm maturing. At other times, I think I will never learn to stop setting myself up to be disappointed by my too high expectations. Certainly, the reality is that I will not always succeed, but the point is that I am moving forward. Comparing my past problem-solving procedures with my current methods, I can definitely see progress.

Although we both were working our individual recovery programs, trying to find an answer to peaceful compatibility, John was still having difficulty separating me from the disease. Through the drinking years, he had become hurt and angry at me, not realizing his pain really concerned my drinking behavior. At times, he took his anger at the disease out on me. Even when I wasn't visibly using alcohol, my "normal" behavior was frequently hostile, so he was confused about where to direct his anger.

In aftercare, my husband learned that detaching, that is, letting go, was the only way to find any tranquility. Sam told him, "John, it's important to understand that detaching doesn't mean that you stop caring about Joann anymore, but it means you are no longer willing to help her die by protecting and enabling." John began to see that, in his quest for peace, it was critical to accept his powerlessness over the past progression of my addiction. Since he couldn't change me, he also needed to accept that in sobriety he could no longer protect me from the consequences of my conduct, change me, or take care of every personal need I might have. Now he had to put *his* personal needs first, and practice saying to himself, "I need to take care of myself first and then, if I'm able, I'll do what I can." It has taken years for my husband to convince himself that it is okay for him to be first. Even now, he still isn't too sure about it. Even more important, he has followed through, learning to let go, as well as working hard to change and increase his own spirituality. Finally, we realized that if we were ever to find lasting peace, we had to allow each other the freedom to be responsible for ourselves.

Neither John nor I are certain what kept us from actualizing our pending separation during the drinking years. However, I do know that hope was a major factor—hope for change, hope for a happier life, hope for peace, hope for spiritual renewal, and hope for loving relationships. It was the persistent hope that God would help our family that kept us alive, until we found the strength to recover from our disease.

It seems unbelievable that we put up with such a desperate living situation for so long before we decided to get help. One day I asked Sam, "Why couldn't we see the insanity that had taken over our family before we finally decided that we didn't deserve to live in a nightmare?"

Sam replied, "Blocking is part of our survival instinct—it protects us from pain we don't know how to handle." This seemed like a logical answer. Today I understand that we had to minimize the insanity in order to endure our so-called life. Also, preoccupation with our individual suffering prevented us from seeing our living hell unfold around us. It didn't seem to occur to us that our life was not a "normal" situation and that not everyone lived in misery.

When I look back at our family life, it's as if I am seeing someone else's family. As I envision myself in the drinking days, it's as if I'm looking at an unrecognizable stranger. At times, I think about the years our family squandered away, and I shudder, as if someone had walked over my grave. If I truly had realized and accepted that death from physical problems, suicide, or an accident was inevitable, then perhaps I would have made my personal decision to recover sooner. On the other hand, my powerful denial had become so strong that probably nothing would have made a difference. The tragedy is that we all lost time that we can never reclaim as a result of the useless charade the disease required us to perform.

Today we know our family is healing when we are able to see some humor regarding the insane times. We realize that part of a peaceful recovery consists of being able to laugh at ourselves and the hundreds of unbelievable things we did to hide a "secret" everyone already knew. In all areas of our marriage John and I have both worked very hard for a loving, peaceful, and happy life, while keeping our sense of humor alive, including not taking ourselves so seriously. It is our firm belief that when we value our relationship and recovery highly, we will work much harder to keep them both solid.

Becoming close to the ones I care about has given me so much serenity and pleasure. Without question, if love and intimacy are lacking in my life, I will waste away inside, losing the inner peace I have finally found. I had to learn *how* to love. Receiving love from others wasn't enough; I also needed to give love in return. Over the years, I found that the more love I share with others, the more love multiplies as it is returned, and the more inner peace I gain.

12

REBUILDING RELATIONSHIPS

I HAD SO MUCH TO DO and so much to undo through my journey of recovery. It was difficult for me to know where to begin restoration work with those I had injured through my drinking behaviors. It wasn't long after I entered treatment before I learned that recovery meant far more than stopping my drinking and making personal changes. As I became involved in AA, the twelve steps of the AA recovery program took on new meaning. Step eight of the twelve steps of AA stresses the importance of listing those I had harmed, the willingness to make amends, and then the follow through, as recommended in step nine. Making amends could no longer be overlooked or minimized if I wanted a successful recovery. Even though it would be painful, it was essential to examine just how many people I had hurt and to set about resolving the pain I had inflicted.

Since I was careful not to drink in my parent's presence, my drinking behavior never caused any problems with them, but I knew our relationship needed a lot of work. All the while I was in treatment my parents were supportive of me and visited me often. Dad even volunteered to make various cupboards for the nurse's station. However, we never once talked about my disease of alcoholism. Anytime I mentioned the word "alcoholic," my parents became uncomfortable and changed the subject. It brought to my attention the fact that our relationship was really superficial. Although I wanted things to be better between us, I wasn't certain how to go about it.

Near the end of my aftercare sessions I had a conference with Sam and finally brought up my concerns. After explaining the ongoing situation, I said, "I just don't know how to talk with my folks. We don't have anything in common and we can't seem to relate to each other on a meaningful level."

Sam had previously witnessed our conversations and agreed that our relationship wasn't the best, but thought things would improve if I attempted to lower barriers in small steps. He suggested, "Why don't you give your parents some informational books or pamphlets on alcoholism? After they read them, you can discuss points covered in the books and lead into more personal conversations."

Without much enthusiasm, I agreed to his suggestion. Even though Sam had great insights most of the time, I secretly thought he had missed it with this particular situation. First of all, my parents rarely read anything other than the newspaper or home improvement magazines, so I doubted if they would even read the literature. And secondly, they were extremely uncomfortable talking about alcoholism, so they probably wouldn't entertain any conversation concerning it. However, I was willing to try anything, so I went along with Sam's suggestion. As it turned out, my predictions held true. Shortly after our meeting I gave my parents a selection of alcoholism information booklets. Then it took me two more weeks to build my courage before I brought up the subject. Their defenses were aroused the instant I mentioned "alcoholic," prompting them to change the topic of conversation. It wasn't until much later in my recovery that I understood that their uncomfortable reactions were the result of believing my alcoholism was their fault.

After my first attempt at improving these relationships had gone down in flames, Sam told me after group one evening, "Don't be discouraged; you can try something else. Lets talk about it."

I thought, "Great, here we go again." His "Lets talk about it" statement inevitably led to more trouble for me. Sam's next suggestion completely blew me away, and it was all I could do to keep from laughing. When his blue eyes crinkled and twinkled before he spoke, I knew I wasn't going to like his plan. He explained, "Since you and your parents have always had problems hugging and expressing love, I think you all need some practice. It will be up to you, Joann, to start the process and to keep repeating it, even if they don't respond."

That man, sometimes I wanted to clobber him. As my bitterness brewed within, I thought, "He never beats around the bush, and without even trying, he always knows how to stir things up." Avoiding my impulse to kick him in the shins, I left the group room. Without much confidence, I went home to contemplate my next strategy.

Although I knew expressing my emotions to Mom and Dad wasn't going to be easy, I tried it the next week, as they were leaving our home following a visit. Hesitating at first, I quickly said while attempting to hug them, "Thanks so much for your support. I love you." Without any verbal response or acknowledgment, other than my dad gruffly telling my mother that they needed to leave, they quickly pulled away from my grasp. My parents were so uncomfortable that they couldn't even look at me when they left the house. Even though I expected that kind of response, it still hurt.

Afraid of more rejection, I waited another few weeks before I attempted my hug and love approach again. The response was no different. The embrace and withdraw contest we engaged in continued for a number of years, becoming more and more discouraging for me. After approximately five years, just when I was about to give it up, there was a slight change. Even though my dad still recoiled from personal contact, my mother attempted to return my hugs once in a while. It felt good, so I didn't give up my pursuit.

Hoping for a breakthrough, I continued practicing hug philosophy through the next several years. As I said "I love you" to my parents, now and then my mother would quickly and quietly say those revered words back to me. In the beginning, it didn't come easy for her. Besides being uncomfortable, she was afraid someone would hear her. On the other hand, my father never once responded with those loving words I longed to hear. Instead, he always withdrew, changing the focus whenever I showed any kind of affection. He was especially difficult, the same as my mom, whenever birthdays came around. When it was time for my dad to open his presents from the family, he became more distant and grouchy, rejecting the gifts. Eventually, I came to dread those unpleasant occasions. It was hard to love my dad. It was especially difficult to tell him "I love you," when he refused to accept any demonstration of my love. Despite it all, something quite remarkable occurred. While I relentlessly expressed my love, my resentments toward him appeared to subside.

Today my father is dead and, although I never received what I wanted from him, my love still lives. Without blame toward them, I can understand and accept that both my parents came from a different time, a different world, and they simply didn't know how to change their old ways. I can now "accept the things I can't change" regarding our relationship and let them go. Through the years, my expression of love has paid off as my mother has altered some. Now she often ends a phone conversation with "I love you," and sometimes she even says it first.

Besides attempting to repair my relations with my parents, I knew I had a great deal of reconstruction to do with my children. So many barriers had grown through the years that I wasn't certain we could tear them all down. In any case, I was going to give it my best attempt.

Immediately after treatment, I tried several times to establish a better relationship with the children, but they didn't respond. Each time I attempted to talk to them, I felt the walls rise up between us. Again I went to Sam for help. In frustration I asked him, "What am I doing wrong? How come they hate me so much? Can't they see I'm trying to change?" He sat there calmly, silently, looking at me with his probing eyes. A feeling of uneasiness came over me, as I sensed the thinking wheels going around in his head, preparing to set me up with some kind of assignment.

Sure enough, he immediately followed through with an excellent zinger. He pointed out to me, "Your kids just don't trust you yet. It's going to take them time. As they witness some long term changes in you, they'll eventually come around. In the meantime, write them each a letter, making amends for all you have done to hurt them, without expecting any specific response." I must say, Sam knew how to wield a sledge hammer reply without even batting an eye.

Completing the letters was no simple task. It took me months to write about the pain, working through my remorse. Every time I started on one of the letters, I could write only a page or two at a time before I ended up in tears of guilt. As I looked over the devastation on paper, it was far more ugly and painful than I wanted to remember. I clearly saw my children immersed in a shroud of heartache and loneliness. It had been a time when we lacked reinforcement of any kind for each other, a time when our love was dying of starvation. It was a period of frustration and anger, of disappointment, sadness, and incredible hurt. It was a time when trust was destroyed and feelings ignored. Looking at the entire picture of devastation became completely overwhelming. With a grieving heart, I wondered, "How can they ever forgive me for all that I have done?"

Finally, I finished my letters, which I now knew by heart. After a few weeks, I could no longer put off approaching the children. By the end of nine days, I had gone to our three children, one by one. Instead of reading my letters, I talked from my heart about our personal losses and my regrets concerning my treatment of them. It was one of the toughest things I have ever done. With my emotions on the verge of surfacing in tears at any moment, I told Renae, Lorene, and Don, separately, "It has taken a long time, but now I understand how helpless and confused you must have been when I was drinking. I can now see you didn't know how to cope with your hurt, or deal with your painful life, or know where to turn for help. I wasn't much good to you during my drinking years, and I feel bad that I was such a terrible mother. Now I realize that I put you in an adult position by giving you too many responsibilities, long before you were ready. I'm sorry that by my poor example and my irresponsible behavior, I taught you how to lie, cover up, make excuses, ignore your feelings, and deny your pain. I know it had to be frightening for you, not to be able to trust anyone with your emotions for so many years. I know saying 'I'm sorry' doesn't erase all the harm I inflicted on you, but I want you to know how I regret, from the depths of my soul, all the hurt I have caused, and for making you live in a hell with no escape. Although I haven't shown you much of my love, I want you to know I have always loved you very much, and my love for you will always be there. I'd like your forgiveness when you're ready, for everything I've done, if not now, then perhaps some day."

Even though I talked to them individually, each of the children were taken aback by my uncharacteristic display of sincerity. As tears flowed down our faces, hesitantly, I reached out to hug each one. Although they didn't reject me, through each child I sensed uncertainty. After a few minutes, our emotions had washed away some of the pain, and a sense of peace touched us all. When I heard each one say, "Mom, I forgive you," my heart was filled with joy and loving emotions. It was our new beginning. With firm determination, I vowed to change our life's course, away from the heartbreaking existence we had lived for too long.

In early recovery I discovered there were other issues that prevented me from being close to our children. For a long time they had observed John and me interacting destructively throughout the progression of the disease. In response, the children had developed similar harmful habits of poor communication, lying, and avoiding feelings. However, first John and I needed to re-establish trust be-

John and Joann's children: Lorene, Renae and Don

tween us before these obstacles could be approached. We accomplished this by demonstrating our example of change with each other. As we instituted openness and honesty, and improved our communication, the children developed more confidence in dealing with their pain.

Even though our relationship improved, the children's faith in me didn't come easily. I realized that there was bigger wedge between us than I suspected. Since I wanted to be a close, understanding, and caring mother, I had to first learn how to be a functioning parent. To better understand that unfamiliar role, I read several books regarding the development of parenting skills. It was amazing how little I knew concerning the basics of raising children and being a mother.

Even though I loved my children deeply, my difficulty in showing them love had always been an obstacle. To overcome this hurdle, I focused on hugging and praising them for their achievements. Since my illustration of sincere affection was completely out of character for me, the children were uncertain about how to respond. After a few weeks of practice, they began to accept my expression of love and gradually reinstated me as their mom.

Through the years, our children conquered various barriers in overcoming their past pain as we redeveloped our relationship. Even though we discussed our differences and worked through a great many problems, I know there are other sensitive issues that have been suppressed for the time being. My hope is that one day our children will become completely aware of how deeply their lives have been influenced by our dysfunctional family system and, in turn, that they will cope more effectively with their emotions.

Even after so many years, the aftermath of the disease still influences our children and their families. The disease reaches long and far, through the many generations of dysfunctional families, my parents, my grandparents, my

Lorene and her husband, Roché

*Lorene and Roché
with their
children: Ikaika,
Talitha and
Kekoa*

great grandparents, each evolving through the years, reproducing the same unhealthy system over and over. During those years, each one of us lived by the rigid rules developed in a preceding generation. In turn, those unhealthy rules were passed on to yet another unsuspecting era, and the dysfunctional dance continued, robbing us of satisfaction in our needs and relationships.

When John and I became parents, like generations before us we also were our children's most influential teachers. Without a doubt, we had a tremendous responsibility to achieve, enlightening our children with what we knew and understood about life. As a result of our past histories, our knowledge and guidance was limited. When I look back, there is no question that I didn't realize what a tremendous obligation being a parent or wife entailed. Therefore, it was inevitable that, when alcohol addiction was introduced into our already dysfunctional family system, certain destruction was to follow.

Through the years, our family has worked hard to resolve our embittered past, and we have healed inside as the pain decreased. Now and again the past raises its ugly head, reminding us of an injury we somehow overlooked, so we deal with it and continue our rebuilding program.

One of my major concerns is that our children and grandchildren are prime candidates to become the addicts of tomorrow. Although no signs are present today, the predisposition of genes is already in place, laying in wait for the chemical to select its next victim. Even though I don't drink anymore, it doesn't mean the illness ceases to exist.

In our family, we recognize that the future well-being of our children and grandchildren needs to be addressed. As I see it, we can intervene with education about the disease, altering the future for our families to come. Informing our children and grandchildren concerning the dangers of experimentation with alcohol and drugs is the best weapon we have. John and I want to give our family

Renae and her husband, Jon, on vacation

Renae and Jon with daughters: Laura, Annie and Rachel

some hope for the future, so we have open discussions about addiction, and we provide various informative alcohol/drug films and books to aid our family.

Fortunately, our family realized before it was too late that our lives and relationships need not be built on chaos and pain. It was wonderful to know that we could actually change the course of our lives toward a more constructive rather than destructive pattern of living. It has made an enormous difference through our healing journey to be able to experience a healthier love, all the while our family relationships mended.

During aftercare, my counselor told me, "It is impossible to reconstruct a relationship on a foundation of anger." He continued, "If we concentrate on punishing others for our pain, our life focus becomes totally distorted, and we end up suffering." He was right about that. Without question, during my drinking days I had become the very thing that I hated to see in other people, angry and vindictive. The fact was, if I continued to hang onto resentments, I risked encouraging my disease of alcoholism to once again be in power.

Throughout the months of aftercare, I realized that the different couples from the various groups had a great many problems. A former patient, Serena, said, "In the past I had difficulty choosing a suitable companion to love. Most of the time I ended up with guys who took advantage of me and my love." She wanted some guidance from the group on how to handle this ongoing problem. Calvin disclosed that he told his wife frequently that he loved her, but more often than not ended up physically abusing her. Then there were several group members who said they loved their partners, but felt no love was received in return. After hearing all this heartache, my problems seemed rather insignificant.

However, as our group discussed these pertinent issues, an interesting fact became apparent. It seemed that

*Don and
his wife,
Tracy,
with their
children:
Christopher,
Andrew
and Mahala*

*Don gives his
niece, Rachel,
a congratula-
tions hug for
winning five
gold medals at
the Olympic
Festival*

no matter how much heartache and abuse occurred in the one-sided relationships, each one still had hope and believed, "that someday . . . maybe . . ." They each had continual faith that the love they desperately wanted would one day be given in return. As a result, several spouses woke up and discovered they had no more love to give their unhealthy relationships. Regretfully, through the next few months, I saw that many of these couples didn't survive the years of destructive living, but then again, looking on the other side, there are a lot of us who did.

Continuing my amends work, in addition to resolving pain with my family, I had several friends to make reparations to concerning embarrassing behavior or remarks made when I had been drinking. Vera was understanding and accepted my apology when I told her, "I'm embarrassed and sorry that I made a spectacle of myself at your party, especially when I fell down your stairs after drinking too much."

Although I remembered most of the demeaning incidents, with others I had memory lapses. Six months before I went into treatment I had borrowed, and never returned, some costume jewelry from my friend Michelle. After treatment, I received an abrupt note from her, asking me to return her jewelry. Thinking she had made a mistake, I searched my drawers and eventually found an unfamiliar necklace and earrings in a bag. Even after I discovered her jewelry, I had no recollection of ever borrowing them from her. Embarrassed about my blackout, I went to her and said, "I'm really sorry, but I didn't realize I had your jewelry." Although I explained that a blackout was a form of amnesia that occurs while under the influence of chemicals, I sensed she didn't quite believe me, nor did she really accept my apology.

The important thing about making amends is to complete the action of making restitution, not to receive forgiveness.

During the few months following treatment, I expressed with each of my other friends regrets over actions and any hurt that I had caused them. After my apologies, we talked through our feelings. Although I was completely wrung out following such heavy work, I felt much better.

Making amends with my friends enabled our friendships to resume, but I was somewhat uncertain about what to do next. Our past involvement generally consisted of the social party scene. If I wanted to stay sober, continually exposing myself to drinking situations with my friends was not considered a good plan. I knew I wasn't strong enough to withstand that kind of pressure indefinitely.

In the beginning of my sobriety, whenever we were in a social atmosphere where drinking was going on, I often felt left out and not a part of my group of friends any longer. Throughout the entire evening I felt tense and afraid that my desire to drink might return. Now I realize that it wasn't healthy for me to test my sobriety in that manner. Being involved in situations that are supportive of my recovery is the best way for me to withstand the powerful influence of the disease.

There were moments during the first months in recovery that were downright miserable. Making amends to my friends and family had turned out to be an enormous task. At times I felt overwhelmed. Other times, as I attempted to change my ingrained conduct and beliefs, I became discouraged. Maybe I was trying to do too much too soon. Inside, I knew part of my problem was that I hadn't completed my amends to my husband. For some reason I was procrastinating, and had saved the most critical resolution as the last one on my list.

I suddenly realized one major stumbling block for John and me was that we were still trying to change each other. At my weekly AA meeting I remember hearing someone say, "You can only change yourself and, as you change yourself, those around you will change their reactions to you." Those were wise words, I thought. Even though I knew from past experience the statement was true, I wondered why was it so difficult for me to follow it through?

Attempting to change myself, instead of others, was completely out of character for me. After some time, I finally concluded that perhaps it was a good idea to avoid attempting to change others, since it usually led to trouble. It was hard to believe, but it actually worked. As I changed my behavior, my husband and children changed their reactions to me. I find it incredible that it took so many years for me to discover this important fact.

Part of recovery, and a major key to freedom from past pain, is forgiveness. Forgiving myself was necessary, and also the most difficult task to initiate. As I came in touch with my remorse concerning my past behaviors, I knew it was time to finally complete my fifth try at writing my amends letter to John. After struggling for two weeks to express what was truly in my heart, my three page letter was finally finished. In one part of my letter I wrote, "To receive forgiveness for all of the pain I have caused you seems too much to ask. Even though there is no way to change the past, I want you to know that I have a deep and genuine sorrow for all of my behaviors."

A lot of my letter was a repeat of what I had talked about with the children. However, there was so much more pain and hurt that it wasn't easy to examine the written pages. One evening after the children were in bed, I told John that I needed to talk with him. He was apprehensive at first, but agreed to listen. As we sat facing each other, I talked about the many painful times, my various suicide attempts, my years of drinking, my continuous arguing and verbal abuse of him, the times I embarrassed him in front of others, my neglect of the family as well as my responsibilities, and my inadequacies as a wife and mother. When I finished accounting my extensive deficiencies and behavior problems, I felt an enormous sadness. With tears blinding my eyes, I added, "I know it's a lot to ask, since you have put up with so much pain from me, but I would like another chance. I want to really work on changing my destructive habits and improving our relationship. We have a lot of years invested, some good and some not so good, but too many years to throw everything away. I know we've lost so much time, and we have tons of work to do repairing our relationship, but I do know for certain that I love you very much, and I'm willing to give our marriage another chance. I know it's a lot to ask, but I want and need your forgiveness when you are ready." Blinking his tears away, John reached out to me, and held me lovingly in his arms. Without any hesitation, he tenderly told me, "I love you too, and I forgive you for everything." He gave me a miracle, much more than I had hoped for. At that moment, it was as if 10,000 pounds had been removed from my shoulders. As we held each other, our past seemed to melt away, and we knew our freedom was near completion.

Though I knew the real tests were yet to come, once our commitment was made, our relationship immediately improved. As I gained new insights and my personal development improved, I seemed to make healthier choices in my daily life and marriage. Now I lived the AA way of one day at a time in both my marriage and recovery.

Once in awhile my regrets over the wasted years would get in my way. When that happened, I reinforced a significant point, "You did the best you could with your limited living skills." After saying the phrase several times, it gave me some comfort. Then there were times when worries about our marriage, our relationship, and the future plagued me. I had to convince myself that even though I might want to know my destiny, I really don't know what mysteries lie before me. All I am able to accomplish is doing the best with whatever resources I have available to me at the moment.

In early recovery, the pain from our past was still raw, so there were times when John and I were inadvertently drawn back into destructive behaviors, as in my drinking days, by something that was said. When this happened, I became discouraged. "Why is mending our relationship so difficult?" I wondered. Our spirits fluctuated considerably, making it hard to find stability in our lives. There were so many unfamiliar changes in my new life—going to AA, going to aftercare, becoming involved in new self-help activities—that at times I was bewildered about what direction I needed to take. Fear that we would slip into our old give-up syndrome kept us both working on improving our relationship. Even though we knew it was going to take extensive work to resolve our conflicts and repair the years of destruction, true to form, I unrealistically expected instant results. My approach to life definitely had to change direction.

During the years of sobriety, John and I, through our faith and ongoing work, have developed a wonderful companionship. Now we could go on a vacation by ourselves for a month and not have a single disagreement. Without daily work pressures, our time is spent becoming close to each other, renewing our friendship. We truly enjoy being with each other, being silly, laughing at ourselves, telling jokes, hugging, and loving each other.

Through the years there have been outside events or people creating pressures, yet John was there offering me support and encouragement. Any time I wavered, his stabilizing strength saw me through the tough moments. Without his love, faith, and patience, I would never have made it this far. No words come even close to expressing how much I love him. It frightens me when I think about almost losing this wonderful man, my best friend. God has been good to me, blessing me with such a gentle, caring, and special person as my husband. I'm thankful that both God and my husband stayed by my side and never lost hope.

For a successful marriage, we have learned that we *both* needed to work on our relationship. Commitment from *both* of us to talk daily about feelings and to have open communication was essential. We *both* realized that it was necessary to compromise, to have tolerance, to apologize, and to admit when we were wrong. *Both* of us have found we can laugh at ourselves and not take everything so seriously. Our relationship is truly a partnership. After all, it is not my assignment, nor John's obligation, to make our marriage work, but it is the responsibility of *both* of us to share equally in our pledge to each other.

13

HEALING LOVE

WHILE ANALYZING certain personal events in my life, I have no problem whatsoever verifying the healing powers that love possesses. One particular illustration of the mysterious mending power of love began to unfold some time ago. In chapter seven I disclosed one of our family secrets, one that our family hadn't discussed in depth for over twenty years. Although we had all thought about her, loving her from afar, our family never dealt with our sorrow concerning the daughter Renae and Jon gave up for adoption. Talking about her brought up too many buried emotions, so it was easier not to open the old wounds of loss.

Nevertheless, all through the years my love kept her alive for me, reserving a warm place for her in my heart. Each year, while wondering what she looked like, I could feel the concealed love offering comfort. Of course, I was curious about her appearance, her height, the color of her eyes, and if she had blond hair like her sisters. In any case, it was too painful to dwell on for long, so I put her in the back of my mind to think about at another time. As the years became ten, then fifteen and over twenty, the prospect of ever seeing her became an obscure dream.

During those years, Renae and Jon had kept in touch with their caseworker, Maggie, at the adoption agency. They had left letters with Maggie filled with love for their daughter. Their other three daughters, Rachel, Laura, and Annie, and John and I, also sent letters, hoping that she would eventually make contact with the agency. In my letter to my granddaughter, I expressed how much I loved her and how difficult it was for all of us to give her up. I wanted her to understand the painful situation at the time, that it wasn't entirely Jon and Renae's choice to let her go, and that both sets of parents had a great deal of concern about their future. I further explained, "After you were born, we were advised not to see you or hold you in the hospital. This was extremely difficult for Renae, not to be able to acknowledge you or touch you. I was with her in the hospital, and we both cried with pain when we said goodbye to you from across the nursery. In our hearts we knew the love for you was there and alive, but we couldn't share it with you. It was as if part of our hearts and souls were torn away from us when we left the hospital. The pain of loss and guilt has never really healed but instead has left an emptiness inside."

Following her twenty-first birthday, and still no word, we decided to pursue another option. Since our eldest granddaughter was now over twenty-one years old, the time had finally come when we could legally search for her.

Among our friends was Al, a private investigator for a local law firm, so we went to him for help. My husband John mischievously said to him, "You know Al, you're always telling us how good you are; now we'd like you to prove it." After relating the details, Al's investigative antenna shot up and we knew he couldn't resist the challenge. Eager to help us, he made some calls, followed a number of leads, and narrowed the search quickly. Within a few weeks Al, living up to his legendary name, "Super Sleuth," had located our granddaughter. However, there was a slight problem. He couldn't tell us the news because Renae and Jon's daughter, Rachel, who was just fifteen, had qualified to swim in the Olympic Trials to be held soon. Al knew that Rachel needed to focus on the Trials, as well as to count on the family's love and support, so he decided to keep his announcement quiet for several more weeks.

Following the excitement of watching Rachel do well at the Olympic Trials, the family met with Al and his wife Eloise when we returned home. Al had previously hinted, "I have some news for you." Even with his brief teaser, we couldn't imagine how great the news really was. Stunned at first, we went wild with elation after he mentioned that he had located her family, knew where she was living, and had talked with her adoptive parents. While joyful tears flowed everywhere, our hearts were revived with intense love as we tried to absorb the incredible report. She even had a name—Julia. Al continued, "Julia is currently preparing for college finals and will graduate in June from Oregon State University. During the past four years she was living only thirty-five miles away. Prior to that time, loving parents raised her, along with her older adopted sister, in a small town near the ocean approximately 150 miles away."

As I absorbed the profile of her history, I marveled at the fantastic miracle. Completely in shock, I had difficulty believing our good fortune at finding Julia. Even though I had faith that Al would eventually find her, I had no idea that it would be quite so soon. Indeed, he was one great super sleuth.

Condensing our story of healing to some important basics—calls were made from Al to the adoption agency and to the adoptive parents, Hal and Jane, and calls were made from the adoptive parents to and from the agency. It was agreed that no contact with Julia would be made until finals were completed and after her parents had told her the news. Our prior fears that she wouldn't want to meet us were soon dispelled when Maggie called Renae and said,

"Julia is eager to meet the family as soon as possible." It was truly fantastic, yet we were apprehensive. What if she didn't like us?

In a few days, after some sleepless nights by everyone involved, arrangements were finalized so all of us could meet Julia, her parents, and her sister, at the agency 115 miles away. Following the long drive, we nervously waited in the lobby of the agency, while Jon changed his shirt in the car for the third time that morning. Shortly after our arrival, we first met with Maggie, the caseworker, then Julia's adoptive parents and sister. We had a few minutes to become acquainted with her open and caring family. Maggie then took Renae and Jon into another room to meet their new-found daughter. After ten minutes or more the caseworker returned, her eyes glistening with tears, and escorted Rachel, Laura, and Annie to meet their newly-obtained sister. While John and I continued visiting with her parents, I tried to keep calm, but I seemed to babble incoherently as I showed Julia's parents and sister the various family photos I had brought. Meanwhile, I anxiously wondered how the reunion was going down the hall. By the time it was our turn to meet our granddaughter, I was a nervous wreck.

When we entered the meeting room and I saw Julia for the first time, I just couldn't believe my eyes. Before us stood this beautiful young woman, who looked so much like the other three girls that there was absolutely no mistake they were sisters. She was tall, slender, with long blond hair and a radiant smile. By this time we were all crying and hugging each other, talking all at once—including the caseworker. It was an extraordinary moment and, without a doubt, one of the most happy, love-filled miracles of my life. The occasion was so moving that we could actually feel the power of love healing each one present in the room. I have never experienced anything quite so touching. Even today, I find it hard to believe this wonderful miracle of God really happened. Without question, the healing power of our love played a vital part in providing a new beginning with one another.

When I think about the tremendous odds against ever finding Julia, I get overwhelmed. The fact that Renae and Jon married and stayed together was a unique circumstance in itself. According to Maggie, in all her years of working with unwed parents, none had ever stayed together. Renae and Jon's powerful love for each other prevented them from giving up their faith that some day they would find their daughter. I tried not to think about the past twenty-some years, and the million "might have's" that disturbed my thoughts, but a few crept into my mind. Julia might have left her family; she could have been married; she might have been on the other side of the country or on another continent. Instead, she was so close—living only a few miles away all these years. In my heart, I know that God kept her safe until it was time for our miracle to unfold completely.

Finding Julia reaffirmed my already strong belief in the power of love. This wonderful experience opened my heart fully and taught me to value love even more. Love is truly the healing touch, soothing the pain through my life. It has been proven to me time and time again. There is nothing like it. My love can't be packaged, or actually seen, but I do know when I have it and how it warms my heart. Each time I say the words "I love you," I feel a radiant, yet peaceful glow inside. Sometimes I wonder if anyone else can see what I am feeling. The wonderful thing about love is that no one can ever take any of my personal loves away from me. The people I love and the cherished moments are my exclusive healing experiences to recall and savor.

Since finding our granddaughter and experiencing the ultimate joy of love's power, I have thought a great deal more about other memorable healing times. Through the years, one major highlight has been being a grandparent. It has provided me with abundant love and a particular joy.

However, I had no idea how much pleasure was involved when I first learned the news that I would become a grand-mother at age forty-three. In fact, I wasn't certain I liked being called "grandma." It was amazing how my outlook changed completely following our grandchild, Rachel's, arrival. A whole new world of love opened up for me. Actually, I decided being a grandparent wasn't all that bad; in fact, it was kind of fun spoiling her with love and gifts. I could play with her, let her mom change her and feed her, let her father change her and dress her, let her grandfather change her and rock her to sleep. Then it was only fitting she went home with her parents and kept them awake all night instead of me. To top it off, buying her clothes and toys her parents couldn't afford at the time gave me a lot of joy. Not such a bad arrangement at all.

With eight more exceptional grandchildren, I experi-enced the same joyful contentment of love. A special bonus is that the love I have found with them is limitless. When

Celebrating granddaughter Rachel's four medals
at the Junior National Swim Meet

each child says, "I love you, Grandma," there is nothing quite so healing and reassuring. Doing things with our grandchildren, sharing exclusive times with them, and watching them grow and develop has been a wonderful experience. In my mind, grandparenting is a lot more rewarding for me than parenting was when our children were babies.

At Christmas, John and I established a tradition of hosting a slumber party for our oldest granddaughters. Early in December they always ask, "When are we having our Christmas party?" When the time arrives, we take in a movie or watch a video and enjoy dinner at a restaurant of their choice. Then we drive around town to see the beautiful Christmas lights, singing carols on the way. To complete the evening, we return home and make Christmas cookies. When it's bedtime, sleeping bags are laid out and John reads the children our traditional Christmas stories. With lots of creativity, we decorate the cookies the next morning, saving some for Christmas dessert.

This custom is a fun and treasured time of love for us all. Not only do our grandchildren look forward to it each year, but so do John and I. One concern is that we aren't sure how we will survive when all ten grandchildren, including Julia, stay over at the same time. Whatever happens, we both know that as they get older, although our tradition will someday change, the wonderful memories and the healing love we share will always be ours to cherish.

Thinking back to when John and I saw our first daughter, Renae, after her birth, I can still remember the feeling of incredible joy that washed over me as I looked at her. In complete wonderment I thought, "How can I feel so much love for this tiny creature?" It was truly remarkable that a mere baby had such a powerful influence. Somehow the strength of love seemed to momentarily block out the excruciating pain of the birth.

The love for my child instilled a desire to attend to the needs of my daughter, whatever they might be. Each time I talked lovingly or touched my daughter with gentleness she responded in delight. It was as if she was letting me know I was doing okay, as well as telling me she loved me too. As I attempted to satisfy Renae's wants with nurturing love, she seemed to be reassured that I loved her. On the other hand, when she felt I deprived her in any way, she cried to get more attention.

After the birth of Lorene and Don, I experienced the same instinctive love spreading through my body, healing the scars of giving birth, while I gazed at each miracle cradled in my arms. I soon found out that our children required constant reaffirming of love in a variety of ways and I wasn't certain how to do this. Although I had plenty of love for each child, I didn't know how express my love. Somehow I felt whatever motherly love I had was being drawn from me, without my knowing how to replenish it.

Therefore, I thought I must be doing something wrong, so I tried harder to meet every need our children had. Clothing and feeding our children, besides offering a home and security for each of them, were ways John and I shared our love. As they grew older, the most desired expression of love craved by our children was to hear us express our love. However, I seemed to have more of a problem than John in expressing love verbally, as well as in giving loving hugs.

Hugging was a form of love and approval that I longed for all my life. Even though I rarely received hugs as a child, when I did, I liked the good feelings I experienced. Although I wanted to, I couldn't say to my parents, "I feel really good inside when you hug me." They would have laughed at me. As a mother and wife, no matter how much I tried, I had difficulty overcoming my insecurities with my parent role enough to satisfy my needs by practicing hugging.

It wasn't until I went to treatment that I fully realized how healing love hugs could be. Following treatment, I began to see more vividly the effects of hugging. Besides feeling a comforting closeness, I discovered that if I hugged my family daily, I witnessed more positive reactions. If I was feeling down, a loving hug helped my depression leave; thereafter, my emotional tensions seemed much less severe. Finally, I found a hug was a powerful and healing medicine that brought alive my soul no matter how discouraging my life situation might appear to be.

During my recovery, I have come across interesting information about the benefits of hugging. Studies have found that hugging helps heal the inner spirit and gives relief to many who suffer sickness resulting from mental illnesses or emotional problems. Hugging has been used therapeutically for centuries and yet I didn't fully understand the influences it provides both physically and emotionally. This new knowledge made me realize how the lack of hugging had affected me.

When I drank, I was depressed, extremely negative, and pessimistic about life a good deal of the time. Since my body and soul were ill, whenever a virus or two was in the neighborhood it would say to the other one, "Look, there's a good specimen, already primed, so we won't have to work so hard," and they would make themselves at home in my body, taking turns adding to my misery. In those days, it seemed like I was regularly seeing the doctor for one reason or another, but despite this, I never seemed to develop any "glamorous" illnesses. Spending two hours in the torture chamber of a proctologist is not my idea of sophistication. It wasn't until I was in recovery that my life and my health began to drastically change. The better I felt about myself emotionally, through loving and caring for myself, the better I felt physically. By practicing the methods of healing love that I learned in treatment, including hugging, everything in my life improved.

Although practicing hugging with my family and my friends was foreign to me in the beginning, it enhanced my personal growth. It was necessary to stop using my fear of rejection as an excuse to avoid being supportive of someone in need. Also, I needed to be able to tell my family and friends, "I need a hug," whenever they weren't aware of my need.

When I brought hugging into my life, I decided to follow AA's philosophy of "one day at a time." For example, one day I hugged one person, then checked out how I felt inside of myself. The next day, I'd take a risk and hug two people, again checking out my internal responses. Each day I increased my healing hugs. At first I felt extremely uncomfortable, but as I practiced giving hugs, they became easier and my barriers diminished.

The following approach helped me a lot:

Eight hugs a day = Recovery
Four hugs a day = Maintenance
Two hugs a day = Compliance
Zero hugs a day = Relapse

It is necessary for me to be wary of the zero area. Today, hugging is a natural part of my life that I wouldn't deprive myself of for anything. Even more important, the healing practice of hugging has increased the quality of love in my family and friendships substantially. Whenever I hug my family and friends, it tells them, "I care about you and accept you." When they hug me, I receive the same comforting message of love.

Because I love myself, I am able to reward myself or take care of myself in a variety of healing ways. When I am hungry I feed myself, sometimes too much. Most of the time when I'm tired or sick with a fever, I go to bed for some rest. I strive to protect myself from harm, wanting to feel good about my life and accomplishments. For the most part, I have no conscious effort to hurt myself, that is, unless I am psychologically unstable, like I was during my drinking days. At that time of crisis, I had no worthwhile feelings and was incapable of seeing any positive options other than death. Yet in recovery, as my emotional strength grew, my suppressed love also returned to heal me. Most of all, I wanted to love and respect myself as I made my life count for something.

During my aftercare, it was pointed out that one of my problem areas was doing things strictly for the happiness of other people and ignoring my own happiness. I had always thought doing for others was the way to get love in return. It seemed my people-pleasing tendencies constantly got in the way of fulfilling my needs in my search for love. To help me, it was suggested that I needed to identify the givers and the takers in our family system. As I explored this, I realized that my mother was a giver of things and good works to the family, rather than a giver of physical love. Even though she continually gave the majority of her generous work efforts to Dad, she received little in return. Mom eventually paid the emotional price, ending up with a great deal of loneliness instead of the love she wanted. This was not the kind of relationship I wanted.

As I examined my relationship with John, I wanted to avoid falling into the enabling practices of the past. I realized that I had trapped myself into the role of the giver years ago without knowing it. Following my mother's example, I thought that if I gave enough, I would find the love I wanted so desperately. As a result, my family expected me to remember birthdays and anniversaries as well as take care of gifts for the various celebrations. When a wedding or graduation invitation arrived, my family anticipated that I would take charge of purchasing an appropriate gift. When I accepted the responsibility without hesitation, I hooked myself. In the beginning it was fun and gave me some satisfaction, but as our family and my responsibilities grew, the pleasure diminished. If there was a family celebration, I became responsible for taking care of the gift, sending the invitations, planning the menu, baking a cake, and cleaning the house. I also organized the games, bought the decorations, put them up, and took care of any other requirements that were needed. Like so many mothers and wives, I thought this was "my job" in life, that it was the road to love. Not only did it take a lot of time, but I eventually developed resentments about "my job."

Though I truly enjoy giving and doing for others, I've learned in recovery that excessive caretaking behavior is not only an unhealthy practice but offers no guarantees of love. Little by little, I have let this go. However, my active husband still relies on me to do the gift buying for special events. In order to make things easier for him, because I know he is a very busy man, I still take care of this sometimes heavy task. (Sounds like enabling, doesn't it?) No doubt it is time for a change. Little does John know that his days are numbered.

In my search for love it was critical to first find out more about myself. This included loving and nurturing myself emotionally, spiritually, and mentally because I am special. I am one of God's gifts, a precious gift that I have been assigned to care for during the time I am blessed with life. In recovery I realized that there is no one in the world who can make this possible but me.

Since exploring the many aspects of healing love and recovery, I discovered that I needed to do some work on taking care of the child part of me, which I had ignored while growing up. I was told so often, "Stop acting like a child," when I *was* a child, that I stifled my little girl desires. The first time it really came to my conscious attention was shortly after treatment, when I was looking for a Minnie Mouse watch for my granddaughter, Laura. As I looked over the jewelry store's selection of watches, an attractive Mickey Mouse watch caught my eye. I had always wanted one as a child. As I looked at the watch, I thought, "Why not get it for myself?" My first inclination was to ignore my desire as frivolous, saying, "You're too old for one." Yet, as I thought about it, I encouraged myself, "Go ahead, you deserve it. Your little girl deserves it." So I bought it; I wear it; I love it, and so does my little girl.

It felt really good to nurture my little girl, so I began to explore the practice in depth. One day, when my friend Lois and I were driving to lunch in her car, I noticed a stuffed bear in the back seat, strapped in a seat belt. She explained, "This is one of my many bear friends. In fact, I have over sixty of them at home." Completely in awe about her nonchalant, doesn't-every-over-sixty-year-old-do-this attitude, I listened intently as she described her bears in loving detail.

Since childhood, I, too, had experienced a warm feeling when in the presence of stuffed bears. It was at that moment that my desire for bears was rekindled. The next time I was in a department store I just happened by the bear section, and lo and behold, a couple of them silently spoke to me with love, "I'm yours; I need you." Giving in to their imploring big brown eyes and soft, cuddly bodies, I bought them. Through the years, I have learned that every bear has its own distinct personality and unique identity. Presently I have around thirty loving friends, most of them gifts from others, ready to comfort me by their healing presence. Even more important, I have realized it's okay to nurture my little girl, to be nice to her, to take care of her neglected needs. It is another special way that I can love and heal my little girl of past loneliness.

Since my needs weren't met by my parents, and I wasn't skilled at being a parent myself, I discovered in recovery that I needed to re-parent myself. By that I mean telling myself, "Joann, you did a good job," whenever the occasion arose. Or saying to myself, "You look great today." Or looking in the mirror and saying, "You are a beautiful person." These are all things I had wanted to hear from my parents, but never did. Now I can say the words to myself, "Joann, I'm proud of you," as a way of giving myself love and encouragement. By taking on the role of my personal parent and expressing all of the words to myself that I wanted to hear as a child, I am re-parenting my inner child. While doing this, I am taking care of my needs, healing myself with love.

At first, being nice to my little girl seemed somewhat strange and uncomfortable. I was quite reluctant to let my family know what I was doing, for fear that they would think I had lost it again. At the same time, as I practiced my nurturing skills, I realized how wonderful and peaceful I felt inside. It was one of the necessary methods that allowed me to heal myself through my journey of recovery.

As John and I worked on healing ourselves and renewing our love, we became more aware of the elements of a healthy, loving relationship. In the past, one problem my low self-image brought about was the importance of always being right. Whenever I was wrong about anything, particularly with my husband, it devastated me and made me feel even more inadequate. In so many situations, we ended up competing with each other instead of complimenting one another. However, in recovery, I realized that as my self-image became healthier, it wasn't necessary for me to be right. In fact, the AA principle of promptly admitting I'm wrong helped me considerably. As I became more confident in developing my own identity and skills, I found I didn't have to compete with John. Without the interference of our continual competition, he was able to develop his own talents as well. While we both worked on the critical area of being more tolerant and tender with each other, it made our relationship much more loving.

Without our competition game going on, we found we refrained from falling into the trap of putting one another down so easily. Instead, I realized that giving strokes of love and care for my husband was much more productive in the long run. When I told him, "You did a great job," his beaming smile told me he liked and needed that kind of healing stroke. I used to think John felt confident about everything, but I have since learned he has many insecurities. He just wasn't comfortable disclosing them. While we worked on our individual recoveries, his confidence grew. One day he told me, with love in his heart, "I need you, and I need to know that you need me." Surprised, I thought he knew I needed him. Discussing it further, apparently I had never told him in specific words, but had assumed he was aware I needed him. So I resolved to be more attentive in verbalizing my thoughts of love and praise. As I learned to give John loving strokes, it made him feel better about himself, and gave him permission to be more open about other insecurities.

At times I become overwhelmed with too much to do. When that is the case, particularly around bill-paying time, I get rather testy. If John picks up on this and has free time, he sometimes offers to take over my job and pay them. When I let my husband know my feelings, by saying, "I really appreciate your taking care of paying the bills this month," I recognize the action as well as the feelings. When we both make an effort to acknowledge rather than take one another for granted, our bond of love grows stronger and stronger.

Another area on which John and I have worked very hard is being more in tune with each other. As we learned to come out of ourselves, we became more trusting of our emotions with each other. When I concentrate on reading John's moods, it helps me be sensitive to his needs and emotions. If he doesn't bring up a problem and I have been paying attention to his body language and moods, I can openly talk about what I see without him becoming defensive. At all times, it is the obligation of both of us to verbalize to each other what our needs are, rather than assume that the other can read minds.

As our love and trust has grown, we feel much safer in disclosing deep feelings to each other. On the other hand, there are times when something is bothering me, but I'm not certain what it is. Yet my distraught actions, or my look of sadness, fear, or anxiety indicates things are not well with me. In the past, I stuffed my problem away, ignoring its existence. Most of the time I was uncertain about how to explain my feelings, since I didn't really know what I was feeling. It has been difficult in recovery to overcome my past habit of keeping silent, of stuffing emotions. The more conscious John and I are of each other, the easier it has been to talk about our various conflicts. Every time we give each other healing and loving support, we ease our burdens and divide our pain. The more honest we are, the more time we take talking on a personal level with each other every day, the better and more complete our loving relationship becomes.

As previously mentioned, both John and I had a great many doubts about whether we could successfully repair our marriage. As we attempted to sort through the obstacles before us, we realized, including the years of chemical addiction, that John and I had spent a long time with each other. We had expended both positive and negative energy during our years together. Even though our marriage was all but legally finished when I received treatment, we made the decision and were willing to give our partnership a chance to recover. We believed that if we worked hard on rebuilding our life together for a specified time, such as a year, and it wasn't productive, then we could decide then whether to end our marriage.

On the other hand, if John and I had separated with the hope of finding happiness with someone else, we undoubtedly would have traded one set of problems for another or, for that matter, the same ones. Also we could get more than we bargained for and become infatuated with another hidden co-dependent or dependent. In addition, we were afraid of risking a repeat of all that heartache again. We felt that, for our sake and for our children, we needed an interval for healing, and we might as well work on it together rather than apart.

Recovery brought alive my obscure hope for a happier marriage and a loving relationship. Although I was sidetracked into an addiction, I never completely lost sight of my search. More than life itself, I wanted to fulfill that burning desire to love and be loved. It was imperative for me to experience the wonderment, the satisfaction, the joy, and the mystery of love as I looked for ways to satisfy my elusive needs.

After treatment, John and I were still trying to decide whether there was any true love left for each other, or if we were just used to being around each other. Yet with renewed determination, as we continued to deal with our disease in recovery, eventually our fragile union began to mend. Although part of the process of our combined recovery consisted of learning to communicate in a loving, positive way, it was necessary for us to search for new understandings about each other that we were previously blind to. It was important to talk about feelings and intimacies that were never possible to disclose when the addiction was in progress. We needed to listen to each other, feel our love, and see beyond ourselves. Recovery required us to be sensitive and nurturing to each other's needs, teaching us how to compromise and work together.

Even through our years of pain, that tiny flicker of love was buried inside of us, underneath our bitterness. Once we dealt with our personal issues, it was revealed and the flame was allowed to grow, giving our love the freedom to develop into the unshakable power that now unites us. The wonderful discovery of giving complete love, of accepting each other unconditionally, gave strength to our devotion to each other. Not only has our love doubled and even tripled, so has our appreciation.

I personally believe that too many couples in recovery lose hope and give up on their relationships far too soon. All who live in addictive unions go through the same doubts and fears about the future. It is my belief that if John and I were able to change our marriage into a loving, healthy, and happy friendship, others can do the same. I often tell those who have given up on reviving loves, not to lose hope. I ask them to remember the repressed love that has been covered in pain for a long time. I reassure them that it is okay to be cautious in trusting again, and unlocking stored love. It's necessary to feel emotionally ready first, before investing in love. Whenever that time comes, personal healing will be evident.

In the course of time, John and I discovered that recovery from this disease is vital for each person in our family, but we needed to remind ourselves that having complete faith in each other again was not going to happen immediately. While our trust grew and wounds mended, the love we so long suppressed had an opportunity to become secure and healthy. We overcame immense obstacles, becoming stronger in ourselves. A new allegiance toward each other developed as a couple. The healing our love generated happened while we encouraged it to grow in a healthier environment.

It became clear that we truly wanted to salvage ourselves and save our marriage, along with our family. We finally learned that the priceless love which bonds our family together definitely needs to be cherished and nurtured always or it will be lost again. Finding the balance of a lasting, healthy love has at times been a difficult undertaking for all of us.

I know now that I can't take those I love for granted, nor can I test their love with my negative behavior. If I choose to create uncertainty and fear around me, then my relationships can never be genuine. The many years that I lived in chaos certainly didn't help me to have a better life or to ease my suffering. Now it was time to choose more successful philosophies of living. If letting go of the past and working the AA program for a new life had worked to bring contentment and happiness to so many others, then I thought, "Perhaps I can have it, too." Now it was my choice to move forward or move backward. No one could make my recovery happen but me.

It has taken so much patience to heal the wounds of this nightmare disease of chemical dependency. Most marriages, like our marriage, where addiction has been present for years, are stressed to the limit. It took many years for our relationship to deteriorate completely, so in reality, it will probably take as much time to totally repair the damage. My belief is that any two people can have a meaningful relationship if they are both willing to work at it. John and I have worked hard and are still working to make our lives better. Today our marriage is stronger and far more complete than I could ever visualize. Our love has returned, greater than ever before. With each passing day our love has risen to new levels of joy. It has become a lasting power and has matured into something very special and beautiful to both of us. We have one of the great miracles in life, the miracle of a special love. It has brought new meaning to our love signature, "Love forever and ever, plus 2 days," which we used from the beginning of our relationship. From the depths of our hearts and souls we know our love is eternal. We can't ask for more commitment to each other than that.

Part Three

Joann giving painting class to grandchildren,
Talitha and Ikaika

14

PERSONAL RECOVERY STEPS

Since becoming an artist some years ago, I learned that there are certain primary elements required to design a painting. First of all, I need a canvas, and an easel to hold the canvas while I paint. Brushes, a palette, various colors of paints, painting mediums, retouch varnish, and brush cleaner are other essential components that assist me when I am creating my masterpiece.

Sitting before the canvas, waiting for inspiration to take hold and guide my brushes doesn't work for me. Instead, an idea must form in my mind prior to sketching it on paper. After deciding the various range of colors I want in the painting, I set up my painting materials. Carefully, I outline my painting on the canvas, using my sketch as a guide before I start my artistic creation.

The most difficult stage of painting for me, though, is looking upon the bare canvas. Uncertain about where to apply the paint first, each time I fear that the painting won't resemble the picture in my mind. I could sit there all day, allowing this blank canvas to inhibit me, if I chose to, or I could walk away from it and do something else. Another choice is to overcome my apprehension and take the first brush stroke. These are all options available to me.

If my fear controls me and I walk away, I will be angry at myself for having no courage. On the other hand, if I take a deep breath, relax my body, and lower my expectations, my painting starts to flow as soon as I pick up my brush. Usually I find that all my worry was unfounded. Therefore, by taking one stage at a time, my brush strokes eventually become a painting.

In many ways, my recovery program is similar to the steps I take in creating a painting. In order for me to have satisfaction in my painting, and my program, I must take certain steps to make them successful. Just as a painting must have specific components to become an art piece, developing a successful maintenance plan in recovery requires certain procedures.

Recovery means changing a destructive lifestyle to one full of positive opportunities. The following pages summarize specific guidelines that have worked for me. Although some have been previously mentioned throughout this book, it is my hope that they may guide you in your recovery adventure.

SUPPORTIVE PEOPLE

Since my former life of addiction consisted of involvement with people who used alcohol, it was necessary for me to seek healthy, non-drinking companions in my new life. I needed to develop a new, strong support system that I could rely on to help me during times of distress. They needed to be not only supportive people, but honest with me and willing to confront me if my behavior was out of line. Not only that, but I had to go to these people when in need, listen to them, and refrain from attempting to handle serious problems by myself. This was not easy to do.

COMMITMENT

When I made my personal vow to deal with my life in a healthy manner, the healing of my emotional, psychological, spiritual, and physical being eventually took place, but it took time and patience. Giving myself excuses to avoid making necessary commitments only fostered setbacks. Therefore I can't afford to procrastinate, but must continue to be firm with myself in my new life. If I truly wanted to take complete control of my life, I discovered that self-change was entirely up to me. I had to face the fact that no one else was able to change what I disliked about my personality but me.

PROBLEM-SOLVING

Throughout my life I didn't know how to deal with any of my problems in a productive, let alone healthy, way. Going around in circles, trying to find solutions to my continuous predicaments was a constant pattern for me. Undoubtedly, opportunities were available to learn how to problem-solve, yet I was unaware of them or afraid to attempt them.

Taking a problem-solving class to learn how to handle my difficulties in a better way was an option I didn't check into. Too often I magnified personal conflicts completely out of proportion. In any event, my problem-solving approach was inadequate and often ended in disaster. I had to make an effort to identify my specific problems, look at the options available to solve the problems, and then make a decision on the most constructive solutions. Now I list the pertinent information on a piece of paper to help me visualize the problem, as well as the solution, more clearly. When I list problems in one column and solutions in another, I am able to see other alternatives, but initially, if I concentrate on keeping my plan as simple as possible, my resolution process is much more effective.

MAKING PLANS

One of the many areas in which I had trouble was making a specific plan and deciding on a precise time to implement the plan. When I am vague about the "someday" plan, it usually doesn't happen. If I include a time frame in my plan, that is, when my project is to start and finish, it is easier for me to follow through with my plans and objectives.

When I drank, I was frequently upset because my plans never developed as I envisioned, so by making plans more flexible, my life is definitely less anxious. However, I have to keep in mind that the more rigid I am when making plans, the more frequently I will end up being disappointed.

GOAL-SETTING

Establishing more realistic goals for myself is another area I often overlooked in early recovery. Whenever I set excessive goals that I am unable to reach, dejection and disillusionment take over and, as a result, I undermine myself and everything that I attempt.

Over and over I set myself up for disappointment by attempting to accomplish more than I was able. In recovery, it was critical for me to establish practical goals, so that I could be more successful and have fewer setbacks. A pitfall for me to be wary of is allowing self-grandiosity, that is, dreaming about impossible goals, to control me.

SELF-RESPECT

Being considerate and good to myself is one of my new recovery goals, so whenever I practice personal kindness, my resourcefulness increases. The better I feel inside, the more I attempt to improve my life. It is essential to remind myself daily that I am a human being who needs loving care.

In all instances, I need to treat my entire being with respect and consideration, just as I would favor close friends. If I handle myself with dignity and with love, others will do the same for me.

Implementing affirmations into my daily recovery program helped me improve my low self-image. By listing several lines of positive messages (specifics are listed in the Workbook section) and repeating those positive messages to myself daily, for at least thirty days, I helped change the way I felt about myself.

CHANGING ATTITUDES

When I make a mistake, I need to avoid magnifying it into a major catastrophe. During my drinking years, if things went wrong I expected more problems to follow, so in recovery it was necessary to change my attitude. There is no question that since developing a more positive attitude, my recovery is more peaceful. In addition, my entire perception of life became more optimistic.

Rather than tell myself, "I can't" change, I replace it with "I will" change. When I say, "I should" do something or "I have to," I experience guilty feelings whenever I don't follow through. It was a big step for me to exchange my "I will try" messages, which encourage setbacks, with "I will do it." Whenever I use the word "try," I am really telling myself, and others, that I won't be successful.

When I substitute negative attitudes with the "I choose" phrase, I take full responsibility for my attitudes. "I choose to be angry," or "I choose to be happy" increases my self-awareness.

DEALING WITH FEELINGS

A vital step in my program is to make a conscious effort to deal with my feelings consistently. Once I become aware of my feelings, I am able to process each of them much more quickly.

We have hundreds of feelings, yet I was oblivious to so many of them. My awareness came alive when I made a feeling list of as many feelings I could think of. After checking out my list daily, I could determine whether I experienced any of the listed feelings. The next step was to decide whether I dealt with the specific feelings or stuffed them inside of myself. Repeating this process each day kept me in tune with my feelings, so it became easier to identify them as well as to talk about them. I am the only one who knows how I feel, so it is my obligation to take care of my feelings in the best possible manner to fully enrich my recovery.

PERSONAL CHOICES

Another critical goal for me is to take responsibility for my own personal choices, no matter what they may be. Too often I blamed others for many of the misfortunes that occurred in my past. Choices are always there, but sometimes I am unable to see them. Instead, when I develop "tunnel vision," it prevents me from seeing different ways to deal with my problems. Even when I feel backed into a corner, I have to remind myself that I always have choices.

POSITIVE MESSAGES

Since I was accustomed to putting myself down, giving myself positive feedback in recovery was not an easy task. Every time I verbalize, internally or externally, unflattering messages to myself, I need to immediately rephrase the message to a positive one. This was and is difficult to do, but overriding my past, pessimistic, internal phrases is the only way to improve my self-image. Even after years of working on my habit, at times the negative recordings get in the way again. Nevertheless, I have to continually be on top of this, ready to activate my constructive messages instead.

QUIET TIME

Very often my life can become so busy and full of projects that I forget to set aside quiet time for myself. Designating a specific time each day is difficult to do but certainly not impossible. My personal well-being depends on how good I am to myself, so I need to include healing time each day, away from the pressures of daily living. In all cases, it is my responsibility to let others know that I want and need the specified time for myself, and then to follow through with my request by actually taking and using the quiet time.

NEW METHODS

Throughout my life I established definite daily routines that I thought were for my personal benefit. Sometimes I became so set in my ways that I didn't want to consider looking at other methods. I didn't like change. Not only did I firmly believe that my way was the best, but I thought others should believe the same way.

My exercise routine consisted of first running on the treadmill, then riding the stationary bicycle, which I followed with weight training, and now and then I spent time on the rowing machine. When my son-in-law, Jon, who has a fitness center, suggested I change my routine for better results, I didn't want to do it. Following the same systematic procedure I had been doing for months was just fine with me, and I had no inclination to change. Sometime after Jon explained why it was more beneficial to alternate my routine, I reluctantly changed my format. He was right, it did make a difference in my fitness goals.

No matter what the issue is, or the definite opinions I have about it, I sometimes get into trouble with others whose views differ. I also have had similar problems with smaller concerns in my life. For example, I believe that toilet tissue needs to roll outward, while my husband grew up with the belief that it should roll from underneath. Whatever the reason for contention, whether it is toilet paper, or something else, some reasonable resolution is required. To avoid a battle for control, John and I needed to learn how to compromise, to give and take, not to demand that everything be in tune with our personal desires.

One practice that helped me was to attempt to do things entirely differently than was customary for one day. If my daily ritual was to get up, brush my teeth, shower, fix my hair, put on my makeup, make my bed, eat my breakfast, and then leave for work, then I needed to mix up the routine or reverse the order. This alteration in schedule may not seem too difficult a pattern to change, but it was hard to reverse something I had become accustomed to doing over a long period of time.

In recovery it is to my benefit to undertake new challenges and to change my set routines, for without change I will regress into my old, unhealthy characteristics.

SETTING LIMITS

At times I have had difficulty setting specific personal limits, in part because I have a tendency, like many alcoholics, to be compulsive. Getting too involved in projects, not knowing how to say no, and over-scheduling myself are areas that steer me toward trouble. By putting into perspective the most important things in my life, I am better able to determine what functions I need to let go of. Making a priority list of my ventures allows my personal traps to be more visible.

For people-pleasers like me, one of life's hardest lessons to grasp is saying "no." Until I practiced saying "no" to the demands of others, I continued to ignore my own needs. However, once I decided what my limits were, it was also necessary to let others know what those limits were. Even when people ask me to do more than my established limit, I must remain steady and follow through with my initial plan.

When I tell someone "no," there is no requirement for me to offer excuses, but be firm and tell the truth. Once I said "no" a few times, it became easier. Another side benefit is that I save time for myself as well as for the party who wants my "yes."

STRESS REDUCTION

One of the reasons I have so much stress in my life is that I often try to cram too many activities into too small a time frame. When I am constantly rushing around from one project to another, I don't have time to take inventory on how my life is going. Not only do I have personal responsibilities that must be taken care of, but other family members, friends, employer, employees, as well as various organizations, invade my space by persuading me to take care of other obligations. If I am feeling overpowered and my life is overpacked with events, then some changes definitely need to be made. If I don't reduce the stress in my life, my entire recovery progress is threatened.

After taking a weekly written check on my current projects and the activities I plan to do in the future, I decide which ones are really indispensable and won't interfere with my recovery program. When I reduce my list by half, my internal pressure also lessens; then I am prepared to relax and take better care of my personal needs.

Doing various breathing relaxation methods for my tight muscles, or music therapy, all reduce my stress level. Besides this, I need to set aside specific time to go for a walk or read a novel and, very important, exercise in some way each day. Since living this quieter, simpler lifestyle, my stress level has greatly reduced.

CONTROLLING

When I am living my disease, that is, displaying old behavior patterns similar to my drinking days, I frequently attempt to control and manipulate the people around me. Trying to change others creates ongoing conflict in my life. Whenever I attempt to control, it's essential to remind myself that I cannot change another person no matter how desperately I try, but I can change how I relate to the person.

Every time I have problems letting go of my controlling actions, it helps if I detach myself from the situation and honestly look at what I am doing from an entirely different perspective. It follows that if I concentrate on taking charge of only my personal needs, plus going to recovery meetings, it helps me to let go.

FORGIVENESS

Sometimes the traumas of my childhood become mixed in with my current problems. A present event may trigger a forgotten memory of my repressed past, or I might come in touch with unresolved grief or anger. If any one of these occur, I must acknowledge my pain and work through the feelings to be free. Each time I come in touch with any suppressed issues, it's a signal for me to reconcile them rather than to ignore them. They won't go away by themselves. If I stuff uncomfortable feelings back inside of myself, my recovery will be harmed.

When I am willing to forgive those who have injured me, I benefit the most, but if I attempt to punish those who have hurt me, I end up hurting myself. Since I carried my emotional pain for so many years, I suffered the most, not those who I thought harmed me.

REWARDS

While my disease was active, I found a variety of unsuitable means, besides alcohol, to reward myself. I used TV or excessive reading as an escape from my world, or often used sweets to comfort my pain. Now that I am in recovery, I make it a practice to search for more healthy rewards and to beware of the old traps.

For a long time I have been a daily list maker, but often my list is unrealistic. It is generally too long, as well as demanding, to finish in one day, let alone two or three days. As a result, I became frustrated because I was unable to achieve my high expectations. Besides this, I rarely put any rewards on my list.

Part of healing is discovering how to have fun without my addiction. Coming from an unhealthy family, I simply did not know how to have a good time, relax, play, or laugh without alcohol. Painting, photography, and tennis were some of my new rewards in recovery. Having a bubble bath at the end of a weary day, or fixing my favorite dish for dinner are other rewards for me. In addition, I need to add several fun things to my list each day. When I remember to reward myself, because I am worth it, my self-image increases. At first, it was hard being good to myself, but after some practice it now feels more natural.

The joy of recovery is not only being free of my addiction, but also being able to be spontaneous. When the internal pressures are removed, I am able to allow my intuitive side to emerge. Also, I need to give myself permission to explore the unknown side, permitting myself the joy of discovering what a special person I am.

PERSONAL STEPS

It is important for me to discuss the specific steps that I practice in my personal enrichment plan. Two vital factors have influenced my recovery immensely. They consist of following the twelve steps of AA faithfully, as well as practicing my individual steps for growth. I have found them both vital to the quality of my continuing recovery.

In the beginning of my sobriety, the major motivating factor for me was intense fear of relapse. As I became involved in my recovery, I saw a great many benefits for both my family and myself. It wasn't long before we discovered there were different stages of rehabilitation.

Along with the strength AA gives my program, the following steps are my personal principles that have helped me in my years of recovery.

1. KEEP RECOVERY/SOBRIETY AS MY NO. 1 PRIORITY

Relearning steps that keep my focus on my number one priority:

1. Become aware of the subconscious messages I give myself.
2. Stop the incoming negative messages.
3. Rephrase the negative messages to positive messages.
4. Repeat, over and over, that my feelings are okay.
5. Reaffirm that I have a right to my feelings.
6. Talk about my feelings with someone I trust.
7. Let my feelings/resentments go.

Each day my recovery/sobriety has to be the number one priority in my life. Without recovery, I do not have sobriety; without sobriety, I do not have recovery. I can't have one without the other, so in order to have a more positive life, I need to be totally involved in my sobriety. What sobriety really means is living the program sober.

My goal to stay sober is far simpler when I follow the program of AA. Fear of relapse keeps me from becoming complacent, so if I am careless, my self-respect, my family, my life, all would be lost to me. When I put myself in jeopardy by not taking the program seriously, or by carelessly testing myself, I risk losing my sobriety.

In early recovery, for some reason I felt I had to test myself and show others how strong I was. I remember my first weekend pass while I was in treatment. John and I went out to dinner and I thought it would be fun to go dancing, too. Unfortunately, the only place available for dancing was a bar. My husband was uneasy and afraid for me to be around alcohol, but I told him confidently there was no problem. Though we danced and had a nice time, I can recall how the place smelled of old cigarettes and stale alcohol, and how there were a few loud people laughing at nothing. When I look back, I realize what a dangerous thing it was to test myself in a drinking atmosphere when I was newly sober and not very stable. If the misfortune to desire a drink came over me and I was in a negative state of mind, I just might have given in to that powerful craving.

Even though going to bars to drink was not a past pattern of mine, what if it had been? If stopping at a bar every night of the week had been customary, I would probably think I could handle it. Perhaps I would be able to for awhile, but eventually, the feeling of not belonging anymore would surface. What if I had a disagreeable day and was feeling sorry for myself? Perhaps I might think that stopping to visit with my jovial friends at the bar would cheer me up.

In comparison, this scene also can have a different effect. I could feel left out, alone, different, not really a part of the crowd any longer. Into my mind pops the memories of the way alcohol once made me feel, along with thoughts that maybe I can have just one drink. The deceitful disease would enslave me once again, tempting me, teasing me, deluding me into believing that I am in control. Perhaps I am able to have my one drink and leave, but ultimately the seed of desire would be sown. It would be natural to rationalize that since I handled it one time, my confidence level would be up, blinding me to any danger, or future problems.

The deceptive power of the disease would continue to work on my subconscious, so when the time for another "test" arrived, I might decide that two or three drinks won't hurt, because I "handled" it before. Even if I am still convinced that I have control, like so many times before I'd be fooled. I would lose and the disease would win.

If I'm not paying attention to my recovery and become complacent, this very thing could happen to me. Even though I haven't used alcohol since I went to treatment many years ago, nor have I had the desire again, I know the disease still has influential authority. Reminding myself that my life is at stake and I have to protect it with everything available, is critical.

My sobriety is a priceless commodity that gains in value with the effort I put into it. I need to guard my sobriety carefully, never ignoring it and never taking it for granted. Above all, it's my responsibility and no one else's to take care of it, nurturing it with loving attention by following my recovery program.

2. DEVELOP SPIRITUAL PEACE

I cannot say enough about the importance of this step for me. After discovering that it was not God who led me down the path of destruction, but myself, life was clearer to me. Finally, I faced the fact that many of my problems were of my own making. No one made me drink, hate myself, attempt suicide, or hide behind by denial for so many years. When I came to the painful understanding that I had no one to blame for my unfortunate choices, my world changed for the better.

In my heart I know that God works in mysterious ways that are not always easy to understand, nudging me here, guiding me there, lovingly showing me the way. However, when I resist direction, I become lost along the way. Now that I have at last found the joys of God's love and peace, my days are fulfilled with unlimited blessings.

For some time now, I have been on God's pathway, free of spiritual spankings, and that feels nice. I feel good about myself as a person, in harmony with my family and with myself. Most of all, I am at peace with God. What more could one ask for?

3. GET INVOLVED IN LIFE

Since chemical addiction is an illness of isolation, I became so preoccupied with the chemical that my family and friends became secondary priorities in my life. By isolating myself, I shut out those around me, preferring to become an intimate friend with alcohol. When it took over my life and progressed rapidly, I found I was truly alone.

Inside, I know that isolation is dangerous for my personal healing, but in early recovery I had to force myself to become involved. After attending several social events, I was able to relax and enjoy myself. Eventually, I discovered that it was possible to have fun without being under the influence of chemicals.

There is no doubt in my mind that if I isolate myself in recovery, I am setting myself up to relapse. Besides commitment to my AA program, participation in my church, being involved with my husband, children, and grandchildren's activities are all important. Becoming active in life rather than just a spectator is an essential part of my recovery. Being a part of Serenity Lane's Alumni organization provided me an avenue of learning how to have fun at a dance or any social gathering without chemicals.

Of course there are occasions when I have to be careful not to overdo my involvement. If I am too involved with social groups, twelve-step groups, or any other organizations, I don't have time to monitor my personal growth. It is extremely easy to fall back into my old pattern of creating a too-busy life.

4. HAVE A STRONG PROGRAM—FOLLOW IT FAITHFULLY

My recovery program needs to be as strong as I can make it. By equipping myself with various recovery guidelines and following through with them, I firmly believe that a healthier future will be provided for me. The primary part of a solid program consists of going to meetings consistently, but I needed to decide on how many meetings a week were beneficial to my recovery. Another tool to assist me is daily reading from the AA "One Day at a Time" book, or some other recovery reading material. In this way, I stay in touch with my inner self each day.

My personal recovery depends on me and how consistent I am. It is my job to achieve my plan for recovery; no one can do this for me. Although my family is supportive of me, they cannot make me stay sober.

5. DISCIPLINE MYSELF—WITH ALL OF MY PLANS

One of the most influential attributes I had to develop in my new life was discipline. Without discipline I won't be able to have a quality program. In order to follow through with my recovery plan and deal with life in general, I need to supervise myself each day.

Whether it is an exercise program, a diet, doing my work well, getting to appointments on time, or going to my meetings, they are all areas where I need determination. Recovery is a program of discipline. Whenever I successfully manage my life, I feel better about myself and my recovery. Changing from an undisciplined life to a disciplined life was very hard for me to accomplish, but as a result, the personal payoffs in my recovery are extremely valuable. Since learning to discipline myself, my self-esteem has soared. My new confidence enables me to attempt other challenges that were mere dreams in the past.

6. HAVE A CONSISTENT RECOVERY PROGRAM

Consistency and discipline are related to each other. I need discipline to be consistent in my life, therefore, if I'm not consistent in my program, then I'm not disciplining myself. For example, if I decide to go to an AA meeting on Tuesday, then I need to firmly commit myself to attend that meeting on an ongoing basis. On the other hand, if I tell myself that I will go to this meeting sometime, or whenever I want to, or only when I feel like it, then there is no consistency in my plan to reclaim my life.

Once I organized my recovery outline and decided on a regular procedure, it was imperative that I refrained from allowing everyday pressures to interfere with the completion of my plan. It is easy to give in to fatigue, over-scheduling, or laziness. Even though I have many daily obstacles to overcome, it is essential not to let them become excuses and interfere with my primary goal of recovery. Being strong in my commitment for a healthy program makes it much easier to be consistent in my daily life.

7. ATTEND SUPPORT MEETINGS REGULARLY

It stands to reason that in order to have a successful plan I need to pay attention to the statistics of those who relapse and those who stay in recovery. If the millions of people in twelve-step programs have maintained their sobriety by regularly attending meetings, then this seems to outweigh the probability of relapse by choosing not to attend meetings. One of the highest priorities of recovery is to stay involved with the winners in the program and not to align with the losers.

How hard I work on my program is determined by how much I want recovery. If I am afraid of having a setback, then I will follow my program more faithfully, but if I minimize my disease, I set myself up for relapse. Recovery is not a simple job. It requires extensive work, time, patience, and being surrounded by the love and support of recovering friends.

8. DON'T GIVE UP

Throughout recovery there have been times when I had doubts, wondering if I would ever make it through life sober. Sometimes fear of the future overwhelms me and clouds my focus of "one day at a time." I had various problems when I was drinking and still have many trials in my sobriety, trials that test my strength and commitment. Sober, coping with life is frequently exhausting as well as challenging.

In the past, I didn't have to face the world without using alcohol to support me. In the beginning of my sober life I realized that the world had not changed, but I had. Today in sobriety I have times, when centering on my unpredictable future, when I feel overpowered and confused. I need to remind myself that whatever problems I am having, it is absolutely vital for me not to give up, not to become discouraged. I must remember at all times that I always have help available for me; I just have to reach out.

No matter how difficult I believe recovery is, the misery of relapse is far more severe. I don't have to give up anymore if I follow my program to the letter. Using my inner strength to deter me from running away when times are tough allows me to avoid the destruction of relapse. If I would only remember, at all times, that I am the one who complicates my life by resisting recovery, it would save me a lot of pain.

9. REACH OUT TO OTHERS

At times, I have difficulty reaching out to others for help. Living in a dysfunctional family for so long taught me to survive a great many problems on my own as I withstood countless pressures. Even though I thought I was a weak person, inside there was amazing strength hidden from my view.

Pride seems to be a primary deterrent to recovery and I needed to learn how to cope with it before it led me into relapse. The statement, "I can't admit I made a mistake—what about my pride?" has led many a person to relapse. What about the person who says, "I am too proud to admit I failed." It is this kind of attitude that is dangerous and can lead me toward relapse.

In recovery meetings, it is said that pride is the number one downfall for chemical dependents. I can believe it. Some of my friends would be alive and in recovery today if they had stopped allowing their pride to rule their lives. Perhaps if they had learned how to reach out and say, "I need help," they would still be here today. If they could have admitted to themselves and others, "I can't do it alone," maybe they would have found the happiness they searched for. What a dreadful waste of human life when so many allow their lives to be destroyed by pride.

Reaching out to others for help and guidance is a major part of my healing. Every time I go to an AA meeting, I am searching for help and for answers. Each time I listen to someone talk about their experiences, I am reaching out asking for help, which contributes to healthy improvement.

If I want a successful recovery, I need to learn how to ask for assistance and direction. When I am having difficulties, it helps protect my sobriety when I call someone in the program to discuss problems. Others are always willing to offer support no matter when I might call. Each time I reach out, I am not only helping myself, but I am allowing the other person to benefit by helping me.

Developing new and meaningful friendships is another form of reaching out that plays a major part in reconstructing my life. When I was drinking, my friendships suffered a great deal and took years to repair, so in recovery, it is vital for me to nurture my friendships constantly and never take them for granted.

Trust in myself and my ability to form close bonds with others has taken some time to develop. In every instance, I had to literally force myself to take some risks in forming new relationships, but once I found true friendships, the rewards were wonderful. One of my dear friends, Ginny, has a great deal of wisdom for one so young. My close friend is very special to me and has helped me in countless ways. Not only do our sincere discussions help me, but her understanding and support at all times cannot be replaced. Along with her sensitivity and insightfulness, she is blessed with a refreshing sense of humor as her mischievous side emerges. When she smiles, her inner beauty and spirit shows in her eyes, lighting her face. Her love and friendship are a real treasure to me.

Another cherished friend, Andy, is spontaneous and full of life. I envy her openness and trust. Her perceptions have helped me in so many ways. No matter what is in her heart, she shares it with uninhibited conviction, allowing her inner radiance to light her entire being. Even on my darkest days she never fails to reach me, raising my sagging spirits with her genuine warmth and love. Her friendship, along with her loving and reassuring nature, means a lot to me.

Other close friends, Tom, with his delightful and direct sense of humor, and Leroy, a gentle, sensitive, and understanding friend, both have been a great support. Also Jim, with his caring and openness, and my warm and honest friends, Diane and Hillary, have all touched my life in many healing ways. All of my special friends have offered their continuous support, wisdom, and friendship to me without question.

Without recovery, I would never have taken the risk of building meaningful friendships. The healing from my disease has allowed me the freedom to reach out to others, to discover the rewards of having understanding and trusted friends. My appreciation to all of them can never be adequately expressed.

10. UNCONDITIONAL LOVE

Since I have come to accept and love myself, I refrain from putting conditions on my love. So it follows that if I don't love and accept myself, I will not be able to offer love and acceptance to others.

When I truly listen to myself interact with family and friends, I can determine whether I am putting conditions on my love. For example, if I give the message to my children that if they don't follow my suggestions I will withdraw my love and acceptance, it is conditional love. If I indicate to my husband that if he relapses and doesn't stop overworking I will no longer love him, it is conditional love. When I put these or any other restrictions on my love, I place barriers between my relationships. In effect, I am not being a loving person to those I say I love. Unconditional love means I do not require any specific conditions of response to my love.

Unconditional love actually declares that I will love you even if you don't do what I want. It also says that I will love you exactly as you are no matter what faults you may have. In all instances, it does not suggest I will allow you to abuse me. It is important not to place conditions on my love, yet I can state the specific behavior that I will accept or not accept.

When I tie strings to my love, I am the one who eventually ties myself up, thus creating the very thing I don't want—hurt and rejection. In early sobriety, I knew that instant trust from my family was unrealistic and I would be hurt if I expected it. Healing takes time, nurturing love takes time, and so does trust take time.

11. PRACTICE PATIENCE

Immediate recovery was an unrealistic vision of mine when I left treatment. Even though I heard the words over and over, "It takes time," I didn't want to believe it. The more I resisted accepting this vital fact, the more problems I had in my recovery.

Most certainly, this is one of the most demanding steps for me. Since I have a "hurry, hurry" type of personality, it is even harder for me to practice patience. I have a tendency to place high expectations on myself, as well as on my family, friends, and those I work with. There is no question that living with too high hopes causes me a lot of pain, so it is critical to lower my anticipations and carry on my search for patience. Stating to myself regularly, "Relax, breathe deep, and be patient," is absolutely necessary. Repeating the statement to myself several times, whenever I experience a perfectionistic attack, helps me a lot. Then it is necessary to follow up with self-talk statements such as "Okay, let it go; it's not that important." When I repeat these phrases, what I am doing is defusing my perfectionistic trait. Practicing this process is absolutely necessary if I am going to learn how to be patient with myself, others, and life itself.

12. SHARE MY RECOVERY

So many people shared a great deal of themselves in order to help me with my recovery. It is impossible to measure the amount of love and reassurance that these people have given me. In any case, my gratitude for their continuous generosity will never end. Without the help of all of these wonderful friends who have touched my life by sharing their lives, I would not be sober today.

When AA tells me I need to "give it away in order to keep it," I believe it is true. "Giving it away" means sharing my recovery with others. Doing just that, in various ways, has provided me with much peace and happiness in return.

After a year of healing, my commitment to help others was as strong as when I first made it in treatment, so I volunteered to work as a nurse's aide at the Center for over a year. Not only was this a rewarding experience for me, but it strengthened my personal mending.

Near the end of that period, my treatment counselor, Sam, who had moved into the position of Director of Treatment, surprised me by asking me if I would be interested in becoming a counselor. Although I was completely amazed by his request, I felt very honored to be asked. After Sam explained how rigorous the training would be, and the years it would take, my old fears started to take over. Backing off, I informed him that I needed to think about it for a few days.

During that interval, I vacillated back and forth in uncertainty. Every time I was close to agreeing to go for it, my fear and doubt overwhelmed me. Even though I wanted to take this decisive step, I was terrified I wouldn't succeed.

So I prayed, asking God to help me make the right choice. Suddenly one day, into my heart came the words, "Fear not, the Lord is with you." After hearing those words, immediately I became calm, my fear was gone, and a complete sense of peace came over me. It was truly remarkable. Then I knew for certain what God wanted me to do, so I accepted the challenge to move into a new stage of life.

Through the years of required education and training, I became more confident in myself and my new goal. During that time, I had to practice my new counseling skills on someone. Of course, my husband was the most likely candidate available, so I proceeded to experiment on him. Invariably, he caught on and told me to stop "playing counselor." Certainly, there were moments when pressures were great and I wondered what form of insanity had possessed me to go into the counseling business. There was so much I didn't know, but whenever I had doubts, I prayed. Following my prayers, the words, "Fear not, the Lord is with you," came to me, along with God's guidance.

After I had my own therapy group, when I began a session, I asked God to show me the way and it always appeared. During the time I worked with patients and families, I saw a need for a more intense involvement of families. I believed they needed a chance to learn how much the disease affected them. Also, it was necessary for them to have an opportunity to start their personal healing. I believed families were entitled to be heard and their pain acknowledged. They definitely needed to experience loving concern from others, along with guidance to care for themselves in a healthier way.

I was not alone with my concerns. Three of us at Serenity Lane saw the same necessity and decided to put together a "Family Program." My friends Sam and Cathy and I worked extremely hard developing our ideas. After countless hours, a strong five-day-long family program emerged. It felt good to be a "pioneer" in the area of family therapy and on the threshold of starting one of the first intensive, week-long family programs in the country. It was an exciting prospect, to offer new beginnings to families in recovery.

A short time later our dream came true. It was apparent that we had a good program and that people were responding to it. Families worked through some of their pain and learned new living skills in the process. They were grateful to be able to have someone listen to them at long last and to show them a way out of devastation. Of course, we knew, and the families knew, that this week was only the beginning for them, but it was a beginning they had never had before.

While being a part of the family program for over eleven years, I benefitted tremendously. As I worked with each family, my own inner healing continued to thrive, which allowed my commitment to recovery to become stronger. The people I assisted have helped me in so many ways. Families offered their trust and their love and in so doing presented me with dedicated resolution and spirit to continue on their path of recovery. In the end, I'm not certain who benefitted the most from the family program, the families I worked with, or me.

The giving and receiving of love, by sharing whatever help and courage I am able to contribute to others, helps me find a peaceful recovery from this disease of chemical dependency. Together with others in recovery is the only way I can defeat the terribly destructive family disease. The bond of recovery aligns all of us with each other, uniting us while we search for life's answers together. By myself I face defeat, maybe death, but definitely I would end up alone in my self-centered attempt to find recovery in my own way.

Today, I fully understand that all of the happiness I want will be mine in recovery and that all of the pain there is will be mine in relapse. Today, I realize that the inner contentment, the love and acceptance I yearn for, is there waiting for me. All of the answers I have looked for throughout my life are available to me, at no cost other than my trust in God and total commitment to my twelve-step programs.

My hope for each person is that you will go to any length for your recovery, make a commitment to reach out to the waiting love, and take hold of this wonderful opportunity for a new life. May it be a life filled with endless fulfillment and newfound peace. May you keep recovery flourishing by finding your path to God. May you trust and practice the proven steps of recovery by living just one day at a time. Believe me, it is worth every precious moment that you spend searching and working for it.

15

RECOVERY EXERCISES

THROUGHOUT THE FOLLOWING PAGES are a variety of exercises designed to assist you in your recovery plan. They consist of specific guidelines that have helped me in my personal recovery. Each exercise has a definite purpose to help enrich the quality of your recovery.

If you use them consistently and practice the exercises on a daily basis, I guarantee that you will see some changes in your life. Using the exercises with an open mind will help you a great deal. If you are able to look at them as a means for personal growth and have fun in the process, they will not seem like they are work.

1. FACTORS THAT HINDER CHANGES IN MYSELF
   (Answer yes or no.)

This exercise was developed to help individuals check on their personal motivation to change. Answer the questions honestly, in order to assist you with some insights into yourself.

1. Am I afraid of not succeeding if I try new things?
   Yes_____ No_____ Comments:

2. Am I uncertain about what to change in my-self?
   Yes_____ No_____ Comments:

3. Have I had problems with self-change in the past?
   Yes_____ No_____ Comments:

4. Is my-self image/self-confidence presently at a low point?
   Yes_____ No_____ Comments:

5. Does my low self-image/self-confidence prevent me from changing?
   Yes_____ No_____ Comments:

6. Do I have problems with procrastinating?
   Yes_____ No_____ Comments:

7. Am I afraid to succeed?
   Yes_____ No_____ Comments:

8. Am I afraid of what people will think if I have a setback?
Yes_____ No_____ Comments:

9. Do I have problems listing my goals and objectives?
Yes_____ No_____ Comments:

10. Are my expectations too high, placing me in a position for setbacks?
Yes_____ No_____ Comments:

Go through each *yes* answer and ask yourself what specifics you can do to change these areas. write down your answers and begin to work on them one at a time.

2. MAKING A CONTRACT

Too often we set out to make a change in ourselves and then do not make a specific plan to achieve our goal. The following exercise is a contract to make with yourself in order to facilitate your personal accomplishment.

Make a contract with yourself or with another person by answering the following questions. When you finish your contract, share it with someone. Set a time limit for completion.

A. What specific thing do I want to change in myself?

_____

B. What do I have to do to make that change happen?

_____

C. Will this change benefit me as a person?

_____

D. Am I willing to follow the steps for personal change?

_____

E. List three obstacles that might be in the way of making the change occur.

_____

_____

_____

F. Set a realistic margin of time to accomplish this change.

_____

G. Have a reward in mind for myself when I have achieved my intended change.

_____

H. Repeat the process for any new change.

3. SELF-TALK

The following statements are intended to be repeated to yourself over and over. They are planned to help you deal more effectively with specific, difficult situations.

These are only a few self-statements to help you move out of an uncomfortable emotional or mental space. Be inventive and make a list of your own self-talk messages.

Remember, it is important to think the words in your mind whenever the need arises. You can handle anything.

1. (when I am feeling anxious and fearful)
   Stay calm, it's not as serious as I think.

2. (when my suppressed anger and resentment are building)
   Breathe deeply, relax my body, then think it through.

3. (when I am feeling threatened by another person)
   Take it easy; it's not a personal matter.

4. (when my feelings are controlling me)
   I am in charge of my feelings; I am in control of myself.

5. (when I am feeling intimidated)
   Stand up for myself and believe in myself.

6. (when I am feeling inadequate)
   I am a good person and I like myself.

7. (when I am defensive)
   Stop reacting and discuss the issues rationally.

8. (when I am afraid)
   Don't panic; talk about my issues and feelings.

9. (when I am hurt)
   I can deal with this, and share it with a friend.

10. (when I am feeling sad)
    Cheer up, life is not as bad as I think.

4. SELF-ESTEEM CHECKLIST

We often do not have a clear vision of our true self. If we grew up in a dysfunctional family, our self-esteem is low. This exercise is developed to help you see yourself more clearly, as well as improve your personal perception.

When you complete the questions, share them with one or two trusted people for feedback.

A. What is my perception of myself?

B. Is it the same as other people view me?

C. What type of person would I like to be?

D. What specific changes do I have to make to be that person?

5. CHANGING NEGATIVE SELF-IMAGE

Most of us are unaware of how negative we are to ourselves. We do not hear the automatic, pessimistic messages we repeat to ourselves each day. In recovery, it is important to change our critical messages to positive ones in order for us to feel better about ourselves as people.

Answer the following questions and practice changing your negative messages to positive ones.

1. List the various negative messages I gave myself today.
   a.
   b.
   c.
   d.
   e.

2. Do I say these messages to myself daily?

3. List some positive messages that would be more helpful.
   a.
   b.
   c.
   d.
   e.

4. Put my positive message list in various locations in my home and at work.

5. Each time I give myself a negative message, look at my list and repeat a positive message.

6. Practice positive messages until they become a habit.

6. SELF-IMAGE CHANGES

Each one of us received either constructive or destructive messages from our parents. These messages have created various influences on our self-image. This exercise is designed to assist you in becoming aware of changes that you can make in your self-image.

A. In what way has my self-image been affected by my parents' expectations?
1.
2.
3.

B. What kinds of messages did I receive from my parents or others that affected my self-image?
1.
2.
3.

C. Did I believe those messages?

D. How can I change those beliefs?
1.
2.
3.

7. PERSONAL SHARING

This exercise is designed to help you have a better understanding concerning yourself. Do the exercise with someone you trust, a spouse, a friend, etc.

Share with each other for approximately five minutes an experience that each of you believes changed the course of each of your lives. It could be a positive or a negative experience that affected your self-image development.

While each of you is sharing, have the other person listen and observe:
- Body language: toe tapping, wringing of hands, etc.
- Tone of voice: soft, loud, harsh
- Facial expression: happy, sad, hurt, angry, fearful
- Eye contact: problems looking at receiver, staring at the floor

Share with each other, for approximately ten minutes each, what your observations were during the disclosures.

8. COMMUNICATION CHECKLIST

So many of us believe that we have good communication skills, when in truth we are extremely inadequate in this area. The following exercise is a personal checklist to help you determine areas of communication that need to be improved.

Ask yourself:
1. Do I have difficulty expressing myself?
   Yes_____ No_____ Comments:

2. Is it hard for me to share my feelings?
   Yes_____ no_____ Comments:

3. Do I get impatient with myself when I have difficulty expressing myself?
   Yes_____ No_____ Comments:

4. Do I have problems listening to others?
   Yes_____ No_____ Comments:

9. IDENTIFYING AND SHARING FEELINGS

It is often difficult to recognize specific feelings, and blocking uncomfortable feelings is common. The following exercise helps us identify feelings we tend to avoid and shows us the personal benefits of discussing feelings.

1. Do I have trouble identifying my feelings?
   Yes_____ No_____

2. What specific feelings are difficult for me to share?
   1.   4.
   2.   5.
   3.   6.

3. Do I feel guilty about some/all of my feelings?
   Yes_____ No_____ Explain:

4. What gets in the way of sharing my feelings with family/others?

5. What is the rule in my family about sharing feelings?

6. Do I believe that *all* of my feelings are ok?
   Yes_____ No_____ Explain:

7. When I share my feelings, do I feel more peaceful inside?
Yes_____ No_____ Explain:

8. What am I afraid will happen if I share my honest feelings?

9. What can I do to change how I feel?
My choices:
A.
B.
C.
D.
E.

10. IMPROVING COMMUNICATION SKILLS

The following list will assist you in improving your present communication skills. It take continuous and conscientious work in order to adapt these new skills. The more you listen to yourself, the more aware you are of the areas that need the most work.

Practice daily:

A. Think before speaking.

B. Talk slowly.

C. Listen to myself:
1. What am I saying?
2. What is my tone of voice?
3. Am I being clear and direct?

D. Be specific and to the point.

E. Don't over-explain.

F. Listen intently when others are speaking.

G. Refrain from interrupting myself and others.

H. Give direct eye contact to the receiver when I am speaking.

I. Check out with the speaker what I heard, if I don't understand.

J. If I become flustered when speaking: stop—inhale deeply—exhale deeply several times—then proceed talking.

K. Tell myself that what I am feeling is important.

L. Refrain from minimizing what I have to say.

M. Don't discount my sharings before or after I share.

N. Refrain from comparing myself to others when they share.

O. Speak in a strong voice.

P. Remember, what I have to say is important.

11. POSITIVE CHARACTERISTICS

This is an exercise to help us come into touch with the many positive qualities each of us has. Too often, we focus on the negative aspects regarding ourselves and our performances. This exercise may be somewhat difficult to implement at first, particularly if you are quite negative toward yourself. Be persistent and complete the exercise with one other person.

(for husbands and wives, sisters and brothers, or friends)

1. Have each person list at least 25 positive characteristics about him/herself on another sheet of paper.

2. Have one person (the sender) share his/her list of 25 characteristics for 10 minutes with the other person (the receiver).

3. Following the sharing, have the receiver look over the senders' list to see if the person shared all of his/her positive characteristics.

4. Reverse the process, (the sender and receiver reverse roles) follow the same procedure as in no. 2 and no. 3.

5. Following the sharing and checking of each other's lists, have each person share for 10 minutes what you learned about yourself, what new insights you gained into yourself.

FOLLOWING THE EXERCISE
If you now feel comfortable sharing with one another, have each one offer to the other person any specific per-

sonal insights you might have gained throughout the interaction.

Be aware of any of your own messages that refer to yourself. If you find yourself being negative, change the message to a positive one immediately.

12. PROJECT PROCRASTINATION

Many times we would like to attempt a new project, but we seem to never get started. This exercise is designed to help you find out what specific problems hinder you from undertaking new ventures.

A. What is the major thing or event that prevents me from starting a project I want to attempt?
   1)

B. What are some of the excuses I give myself to avoid starting a project?
   1)
   2)
   3)

C. What steps do I need to take in order to overcome my procrastination?
   1)
   2)
   3)

D. Once I determine what my obstacles are, ask myself: What is the worst thing that can happen if my project is not as successful as I anticipate?

E. Ask myself: Will I be able to accept this if the outcome is not successful?
   Yes_____ No_____

F. If my answer is yes, start my project. If my answer is no, repeat the steps again to make certain that I understand them fully.

13. GOAL-PLANNING

Sometimes we have a goal we would like to achieve, but we are not certain how to make this happen. Frequently we do not know how to set up the steps to achieve our goals. The following exercise is intended to train you to think in terms of "steps" when you first decide that you want to achieve a goal.

Follow this procedure for each of your goals:

1. Write down a future goal (long-range or short-range) that I intend to achieve.

2. Complete the steps below in order to achieve this goal.
   a) What is the goal?

   b) What do I need to do to achieve the goal?
      1.

      2.

      3.

   c) When will I start the goal?
      Date:
      Time:

d)   When will I complete the goal?
      Date:
      Time:

14. GOAL-ACHIEVING

The following exercise is meant to help you decide on a particular goal that you would like to achieve. It is also designed to help you become aware of inner feelings surrounding goal achievement.

A. Is there a particular goal that I would like to achieve?

_____

_____

B. What stops me from achieving this goal?

_____

_____

C. How do I feel about myself when I procrastinate?

_____

_____

D. What can I do to motivate myself to achieve my goals?

_____

_____

15. REWARDS LIST

In recovery, we live our lives without the chemicals that used to be our primary personal reward. Whether you are a dependent or co-dependent, it is important that you learn to reward yourself in positive ways. Too often we neglect to add rewards to our daily "to do" lists. Add at least two rewards per day to your list.

Listed below are some possible rewards for yourself. Add your personal rewards and implement them in your daily life.

1) Take a walk.   9)

2) Go to a movie.   10)

3) Take a nap.   11)

4) Listen to music.   12)

5) Relax in a bubble bath. 13)

6) Read a book.   14)

7)   15)

8)   16)

16. EXPRESSING FEELINGS

Frequently we have difficulty expressing our feelings. This exercise is aimed at helping you identify and express your feelings.

When I am confused about why I am feeling negative:

A. Identify and write down the feelings I am experiencing at the moment.

1.   4.
2.   5.
3.   6.

FEELING GUIDE:

joy	nervousness	_____
fear	happiness	_____
anger	love	_____
hurt	confusion	_____
shyness	frustration	_____
sadness	anxiety	_____
helplessness	hopelessness	_____
insecurity	suspiciousness	_____
hostility	fright	_____
guilt	_____	_____
_____	_____	_____
_____	_____	_____

C. Are these feelings that I have neglected to deal with?
Yes_____ No_____

D. Do I accept these feelings as valid feelings?
Yes_____ No_____

E. Do I accept that I have a right to these
   feelings?
   Yes_____ No_____

F. Talk about the feelings with someone close to
   me.

G. Tell myself that I will not allow my feelings to
   control me.

H. Let go of the feelings.

17. DEFENSE MECHANISMS

*Defense mechanisms are barriers that we automatically put
up when we are threatened in some way. Each person has various
defense mechanisms. It is important to identify the personal defense
mechanisms that you have problems with.*

Listed below are some common defense mechanisms.
Circle the ones I have problems with.

* Justifying	* Arguing
* Minimizing	* Lying
* Judging	* Manipulating
* Smiling	* Shouting
* Leaving	* Ignoring
* Attacking	* Silence
* Withdrawing	* Analyzing
* Intellectualizing	* Blaming
* Explaining	* Threatening
* Defying	* Talking
* Rationalizing	

Following identification, make a daily checklist of
defense mechanisms that I use during the day, and how

often I use each one. Focus on three that I have the most difficulty with. As my self-awareness grows, attempt to reduce the times I use my defense mechanisms.

18. STEPS TO A FULFILLING RECOVERY

Listed below are the basic healthy steps to help you to have a more fulfilling and peaceful recovery. Keep in mind and follow all of the steps to reinforce your recovery.

For a fulfilling, peaceful recovery, I must:
1) Be kind to myself.
2) Be honest with myself.
3) Identify and discuss my feelings daily.
4) Accept myself for what I am.
5) Give myself permission to make mistakes.
6) Find new methods to do things in my life.
7) Stop negative self-talk.
8) Take responsibility for my actions.
9) Trust my instincts.
10) Set personal limits and boundaries.
11) Forgive myself and others.

19. DEALING WITH GRIEF ISSUES

Many of us do not know how to deal with grief. We tend to shut down the process because it is so painful. Whether our grief concerns a death, a divorce, a move, a loss of a job, etc., it is extremely important for us to work through our grief and not leave it unfinished.

The following exercise is a guideline to assist me in starting to deal with my grief issues.

1) Recognize the feelings—circle the feelings I am experiencing.

   a. anger   f. loneliness
   b. relief   g. _____
   c. helplessness   h. _____
   d. guilt   i. _____
   e. sadness   j. _____

2) Talk about the pain:
   a. with someone I trust.
   b. with family.
   c. with a friend.
   d. with a minister.
   e. with a counselor.

3) Write the person I am grieving about a letter, sharing the things that I didn't get a chance to share.

4) Share the letter with a counselor or minister, someone who can help me work through my emotions.

5) Say my goodbyes:
   a. in my heart.
   b. verbally with my counselor, etc.
   c. in a letter.

6) Tell myself to let the person go, until I feel at peace inside.

20. GOAL PLAN 1

In order to reach our goals more effectively, we need to make a plan and put it into small steps. Remember, on a stairway you cannot go from the bottom of the steps to the top without taking the steps in between. The same principle applies when setting either long term or short term goals.

Implement my plan by going from step to step until I reach my ultimate goal.

EXAMPLE:

If I want to lose 15 lbs., it is unrealistic to think that this weight will be eliminated the first day of my diet. Devise a plan on paper, with smaller steps of losing 1 or 2 lbs. per week, until I reach my final goal.

WEEK	GOAL	WEIGHT
week 1	2 lbs.	_____
week 2	2 lbs.	_____
week 3	_____	_____
week 4	_____	_____
week 5	_____	_____
week 6	_____	_____
TOTAL LBS. LOST:		_____

21. GOAL PLAN 2

Follow the same process as the above exercise for attaining other goals.

EXAMPLE:
If I wish to tone up my body and lose weight, vary my exercise routines. If I attempt to do too much during the first week, I am in danger of doing injury to myself, becoming fatigued, and giving up. Take it slow; be patient.

WEEK	EXERCISE	TIME
week 1	walking	10 min.
week 2	acrobics	20 min.
week 3	jogging	30 min.
week 4	_____	_____
week 5	_____	_____
week 6	_____	_____

22. RELIEVING STRESS

The following list consists of ways to eliminate stress in your life. Use all of these techniques or as many as you are able to so that you will reduce the effects of your particular pressures.

A. Learn relaxation techniques, such as:
1. deep breathing.
2. muscle relaxation.
3. sleep.
4. meditation.

B. Listen to relaxation tapes, such as:
1. music.
2. soothing voices, guided relaxation/imagery.
3. ocean/surf sounds.
4. birds/wind sounds.

C. Reduce stress at work—change my workload.
   1. Delegate to others.
   2. Learn time management.
   3. Exercise/deep breathe at your job site.

D. Do physical exercise daily.
   1. racquetball   5. tennis
   2. brisk walking   6. jogging
   3. bicycling   7. _____
   4. swimming   8. _____

E. Change my pace.
   1. Do something different, get out of my rut.
   2. Spend a long, quiet weekend out of town.
   3. Get a massage.
   4. Go to a funny movie.
   5. Read a book.
   6. Visit the elderly.

F. Talk about my various stressors:
   1. with my family.
   2. with a close friend.
   3. with a counselor.
   4. in a self-help group.

23. AFFIRMATIONS

Making affirmations means giving ourselves positive and reinforcing messages. Repeating affirmations daily is an important tool in building a positive self-image.

EXAMPLE:
Look into the mirror for thirty days and say ten times each day:
"I am a beautiful person."

EXAMPLE:

Look into the mirror for thirty days and say each phrase five times—twice a day:

"I like myself."

"I do not expect to be perfect."

"I accept myself for what I am."

24. FAMILY CONFERENCE

Families often have difficulty in really communicating with each other. Setting aside time when everyone can be together is extremely hard, but not impossible. The family conference format is very important in assisting families with sharing their feelings and problems and in learning to listen to each other. I have seen many families unite together by using this format on a consistent weekly basis.

Find a weekly time and day when the family can sit down together for an hour. Each person has an opportunity to share and listen throughout the meeting. The session is not intended to be a time for attacking, griping, arguing or blaming. Stick to the format, sharing only personal feelings and thoughts.

It is important that everyone be given a chance to express themselves without help or interference from one another. Each week select a new leader to conduct the conference to see that the meeting starts and stops on time, and that order is followed.

1. What kinds of things have been bothering me? What are my feelings about them?

2. Do I have some specific fears that concern me?

3. Do I need some answers from anyone regarding questions I might have?

4. Do I have something nice or complimentary to share with someone?

25. MAINTAINING PROGRESS

Frequently we get lazy in implementing our recovery program on a consistent basis. Listed below are some helpful steps to assist you in keeping your progress on a healthy level.

A. Do something each day to help improve my self-image.

B. Deal with my feelings daily.

C. Update my inventory monthly.

D. Set realistic, attainable goals.

E. Tell myself that "I will do," rather than "I'll try." Tell myself that "I am going to" rather than "I'll try."

F. Attempt new things; make new decisions.

G. Reward myself each day.

H. Take care of my personal needs.

I. Take care of my emotional needs.

26. PERSONAL CARE OF MYSELF

Caretakers of the world have a difficult time concentrating on taking care of themselves. This exercise is intended to help you focus on the various personal steps to help you take care of yourself on a consistent basis.

Steps for personal care of myself:

A. Practice "HALT":
   Don't get too Hungry.
   Don't get too Angry.
   Don't get too Lonely.
   Don't get too Tired.

B. Pay attention to a healthy diet.

C. Find methods to reduce stress.
   1. Read.
   2. Listen to music.
   3. Do muscle-relaxation therapy.
   4. Listen to relaxation therapy tapes.
   5. Exercise regularly.

D. Get enough rest, relaxation, and sleep.

E. Exercise on a consistent basis.

F. Take care of my personal hygiene.

G. Practice self-discipline daily.

H. Refrain from over-scheduling, doing too much.

I. Concentrate on my successes and not on my setbacks.

J. Learn to say "No," if my pattern is to always say "Yes."

K. Reward myself daily.

L. Make a "fun list" and use it daily.

27. STEPS TO HEALING

There are times when we are unable to find the answers to our problems on our own. Reaching out to others or finding professional help are other methods of obtaining help. Listed below are some guidelines to assist in finding other sources to help heal ourselves in recovery.

1. Attend my twelve-step meetings regularly and weekly.
2. Involve myself in a specialized therapy group.
3. Spend some quiet time meditating each day.
4. Find a sponsor, a counselor, a friend, or a minister to share my problems with.
5. Deal with my past, so I can live today.
6. Learn to forgive myself and others.
7. Be honest with myself and others.
8. Stop controlling others.
9. Work on changing myself only.
10. Take responsibility for my life only.
11. Listen to the wisdom of others.
12. Find spiritual peace and happiness.

28. CHANGING NEGATIVE TAPES

Think about the last time you felt a sense of rejection from someone close to you. What was your reaction? Were you angry or hurt? Did you feel it might have been your fault, something you had done to cause this rejection? If you answered "yes" to these questions, yours is a most common reaction. Putting ourselves down, blaming ourselves, is a natural response for those of us who grew up in dysfunctional families. For many of us, every time we are denied the personal satisfaction we experience following an accomplishment, we tend to put ourselves down in self-defeating ways.

EXAMPLE:
Following a mistake, if you say to yourself:
"You stupid jerk, how dumb can you be?" or
"I can't believe you can be so stupid, you're a real jerk."

As soon as you hear this automatic statement by your inner voice, change the message to:
"I made a mistake; it's okay, I'll do better next time."

Can you see the different connotations of each message? The first one is debilitating and very destructive to your self-image. Every time you give your self this negative input, your self-image deteriorates more.

Keep in mind that the second message does not chastise you for a mistake. It acknowledges your error yet gives you permission. Then, the reinforcing part, "I'll do better (not perfect, but better) next time," gives you a morale booster. The more positive messages you give yourself, the better you will feel about yourself.

29. CHILDREN'S AFFIRMATIONS

• Put this paper on your mirror in the bathroom, or in your bedroom.
• Look at yourself in the mirror and repeat the affirmations out loud 3 or 4 times.
• Say your affirmations when you wake up in the morning, when you go to bed, and during the day.

I like myself.
I am a special person.
I don't criticize myself—I accept myself as I am.
I have a right to my feelings.

30. CHILDREN'S FEELINGS EXERCISE

1. I give myself permission to *feel every feeling.*

2. I don't put myself down for any feeling.

3. Accepting my feelings means accepting myself.

4. My behavior is a reaction to my feelings:
   A. anger   violence
   B. fear   running away
   C. guilt   punishment
   D. sadness   _____
   E. happiness   _____
   F. worry   _____
   G. stupidity   _____
   H. confusion   _____
   I. loneliness   _____
   J. rejection   _____
   K. depression   _____
   L. hurt   _____
   M. love   _____
   N. hopelessness   _____

O. frustration   _____
P. insecurity   _____
Q. distrust   _____
R. resentment   _____
S. embarrassment   _____
T. worry   _____
U. inferiority   _____
V. unimportance   _____
W. abandonment   _____
X. _____   _____
Y. _____   _____
Z. _____   _____

5. My feelings and my behavior are not the same thing.

6. I can *choose* how I feel.

7. I can *choose* how I react to my feelings.

8. I can *choose* new, positive behavior as I react to my feelings, such as:
   * Talking
   * Exercising
   * Drawing
   * Writing

9. I am responsible for how I feel.

10. No one else is responsible for how I feel.

11. I need to stop blaming others for how I feel.

12. I need to share my feelings with another person.

13. Feelings that I do not share don't go away by themselves.

14. When I don't deal with my feelings, they build up inside of me and make me sick.

15. Learning to share my feelings when I am aware of them is important so that I can feel better as a person.

16. After I talk about my feelings, I need to let my feelings go—so they won't upset me anymore.

17. I need to remind myself often that *my feelings are okay and that they are neither right nor wrong.*

18. I need to remind myself that *I am human, and have problems, just like every human being.*

19. I need to stop putting myself down for my feelings, and, in fact, recognize all my feelings.

20. I need to remind myself that I am a good person who has human feelings.

Alcoholics Anonymous
12 Step Program of Recovery

THE FOLLOWING ARE THE 12 steps of Alcoholics Anonymous. These same steps are used as a basis for hundreds of other support and recovery programs. Note that only the first and last steps mention anything about alcohol. The rest dictate a healthy approach to clearing the wreckage of the past.

1. We admitted we were powerless over alcohol and our lives had become unmanageable.
2. Came to believe that a Power greater than ourselves could restore us to sanity.
3. Made a decision to turn our will and our lives over to the care of God as we understood Him.
4. Made a searching and fearless inventory of ourselves.
5. Admitted to God, to ourselves, and to another human being the exact nature of our wrongs.
6. Were entirely ready to have God remove all these defects of character.
7. Humbly asked him to remove our shortcomings.
8. Made a list of all persons we had harmed, and became willing to make amends to them all.
9. Made direct amends to such people wherever possible, except when to do so would injure them or others.
10. Continued to take personal inventory and when we were wrong promptly admitted it.
11. Sought through prayer and meditation to improve our conscious contact with God as we understood Him, praying only for knowledge of His will for us and the power to carry it out.
12. Having had a spiritual awakening as a result of these steps, we tried to carry this message to alcoholics, and to practice these principles in all our affairs.

SUGGESTED READING

ALCOHOLICS ANONYMOUS, *The Big Book*
New York, NY
ALCOHOLICS ANONYMOUS, *12 Steps—12 Traditions*
New York, NY
MELODIE BEATTIE, *Beyond Codependency*
Center City, MN: Hazeldon.
CLAUDIA BLACK, *It Will Never Happen To Me*
Denver, CO: M.A.C. Printing & Publishing
DOUGLAS BLOCH, *Words That Heal*
New York, NY: Bantam Books
JOANN BREEDEN, *Chemical Family*
Eugene, OR: Serenity Lane Treatment Center
STEPHANIE BROWN, *Safe Passage*
New York, NY: John Wiley & Sons
HELEN COULTON, *Touch Therapy*
Putnam & Zebra Books
SHARON WEGSCHEIDER-CRUSE, *Another Chance*
Palo Alto, CA: Science & Behavior Books, Inc.
ELAINE FORD, *Betty*
New York, NY: Doubleday & Co., Inc.
WILLIAM GLASSER, *Reality Therapy*
San Francisco, CA: Harper & Row Publishers
WILLIAM GLASSER, *Control Theory*
San Francisco, CA: Harper & Row Publishers
VERNON E. JOHNSON, *I'll Quit Tomorrow*
San Francisco, CA: Harper & Row Publishers

ABOUT THE AUTHOR

JOANN BREEDEN IS A RECOVERYING ALCOHOLIC with over nineteen years of sobriety. Following treatment in 1974 at Serenity Lane, a treatment center for addiction and co-dependency, in Eugene, Oregon, she volunteered at the center for one year as a nurse's aide. After extensive counseling training, she became a Certified Addiction Counselor, working over seventeen years counseling alcoholics/addicts and their families, with a focus on children and co-dependents' issues. She was co-founder of Serenity Lane's Family Program in 1977 and co-supervised the program for eleven years, gaining experience in areas of intervention, lecturing, teaching, and management of chemical dependency and co-dependency treatment. In 1984 she wrote a 34-page book entitled *Chemical Family*. The book is primarily clinical and covers the specific roles and behavior patterns developed in a chemical family system.

Currently Joann is Director of Family Education Services at Serenity Lane Health Services, where she organizes, presents, and manages one-day recovery workshops and five-day intensive workshop/groups designed to help those in recovery and their families.

The five-day workshop/groups cover advanced communication skills, self-esteem, and grief work. Among the many issues addressed are control problems, enabling and co-dependency, family-of-origin concerns, relaxation therapy, and healthy recovery guidelines. (For further information about these and other programs, contact Serenity Lane, 616 E. 16th, Eugene, OR 97401, phone (503) 687-1110.)

In addition to the workshops, Joann presents lectures at the treatment center, schools, and churches in the community. She attended Dr. William Glasser's Reality Therapy Institute and has had training in psychodrama, psychotherapy, relaxation therapy, adolescent and co-dependency treatment. She also attended the University of Washington School of Social Work and Sierra Tucson Grief Therapy for special training. Each year Joann attends workshops and trainings concerning current treatment issues, family therapy, and counseling techniques.